BASIC / NOT BORING
SCIENCE SKILLS

EARTH & SPACE
SCIENCE

Grades 6–8[+]

Inventive Exercises to Sharpen
Skills and Raise Achievement

Series Concept & Development
by Imogene Forte & Marjorie Frank
Exercises by Marjorie Frank

Incentive Publications, Inc.
Nashville, Tennessee

About the cover:
   Bound resist, or tie dye, is the most ancient known method
   of fabric surface design. The brilliance of the basic tie dye
   design on this cover reflects the possibilities that emerge
   from the mastery of basic skills.

Illustrated by Kathleen Bullock
Cover art by Mary Patricia Deprez, dba Tye Dye Mary®
Cover design by Marta Drayton, Joe Shibley, and W. Paul Nance
Edited by Anna Quinn

ISBN 0-86530-375-4

PRINTED IN THE UNITED STATES OF AMERICA

TABLE OF CONTENTS

CELEBRATE BASIC
EARTH & SPACE SCIENCE SKILLS

Basic does not mean boring! There certainly is nothing dull about . . .

 . . . visiting with viruses

 . . . wondering whether the weather you're in is a cyclone, hurricane, tornado, or waterspout

 . . . tracking down some of the world's shakiest earthquakes and wildest volcanic eruptions

 . . . getting a sense of the great jigsaw puzzle that makes up Earth's surface

 . . . exploring coral reefs, ocean trenches, underwater mountain ranges, and other wonders beneath the sea

 . . . looking into glaciers, mudpots, geysers, caves, ice shelves, volcanic craters, and other wonders above the surface

 . . . adventuring around outer space with comets, meteors, meteorites, shooting stars, asteroids, and other space wanderers

 . . . becoming an expert on moon phases, eclipses, and tides

The idea of celebrating the basics is just what it sounds like—getting excited about science because you understand more about how things work. The pages that follow are full of exercises for students that will help to **review and strengthen specific, basic skills in the content area of earth and space science.** This is not just another ordinary "fill-in-the-blanks" way to learn. The high-interest exercises will put students to work applying a rich variety of the most important facts about earth and outer space while enjoying fun and challenging exercises.

The pages in this book can be used in many ways:
 • for individual students to sharpen a particular skill
 • with a small group needing to relearn or strengthen a skill
 • as an instructional tool for teaching a skill to any size group
 • by students working on their own
 • by students working under the direction of an adult

Each page may be used to introduce a new skill or content area, reinforce a skill, or assess a student's ability to perform a skill. And, there's more than just the great student activities! You'll also find a hearty appendix of resources helpful for students and teachers—including a ready-to-use test for assessing these earth and space science content skills.

As students take on the challenges of these adventures with wonders in the world and outer space, they will sharpen their mastery of basic skills and will enjoy learning to the fullest. And as you watch them check off the basic earth and space science skills they've strengthened, you can celebrate with them!

SKILLS CHECKLIST FOR EARTH & SPACE SCIENCE

✔	SKILL	PAGE(S)
	Describe and draw a model of the solar system	10, 11
	Identify, describe, and compare characteristics of each planet	10, 11, 12
	Define and describe features of stellar astronomy	13
	Define and describe characteristics of other objects in the solar system	14
	Define, describe, and differentiate among movements of objects in space	15, 16, 17
	Explain seasons, equinox, and solstice	16
	Describe and diagram the moon's phases and motions	17
	Describe and diagram lunar and solar eclipses	18
	Define and describe several tools of space exploration and travel	19
	Identify major accomplishments and events in space exploration	20, 21
	Define, describe, and diagram Earth's atmosphere	22
	Define, describe, and illustrate different winds and Earth air movements	23
	Define weather and describe factors that contribute to it	24, 25, 26
	Describe and distinguish among different kinds of weather fronts	26
	Identify and describe a variety of weather patterns	24, 25, 26
	Define and distinguish among different kinds of precipitation	24, 25, 26
	Describe factors that influence climate; list classifications of climate	27, 28
	Define and use vocabulary terms related to weather and climate	24-28
	Describe and define different motions of the ocean	30, 31, 32, 33
	Diagram and describe parts and motions of an ocean wave	31
	Explain and diagram causes of high, low, neap, and spring tides	33
	Diagram and describe characteristics of the ocean floor	34
	Define weathering and erosion; explain agents and examples of each	35-39
	Describe effects and processes of wind erosion	35
	Describe effects and processes of water erosion	35, 36, 37
	Define and describe characteristics of rivers and riverbeds	36, 37
	Define and describe actions and features formed by groundwater	38
	Identify and compare kinds and effects of glaciers	39
	List and define characteristics used to identify minerals	44, 45
	Identify and distinguish among common minerals	44, 45
	Define and explain formation of three classes of rocks	42, 43
	Identify and describe layers and features of the earth's crust	40
	Identify and describe various landforms on the earth	41, 50
	Define and illustrate terms and processes related to earthquakes and plate tectonics	47, 48, 49
	Identify features related to volcanoes	46, 49
	Investigate some of the earth's most notable earthquakes and volcanoes	49

EARTH & SPACE SCIENCE

Skills Exercises

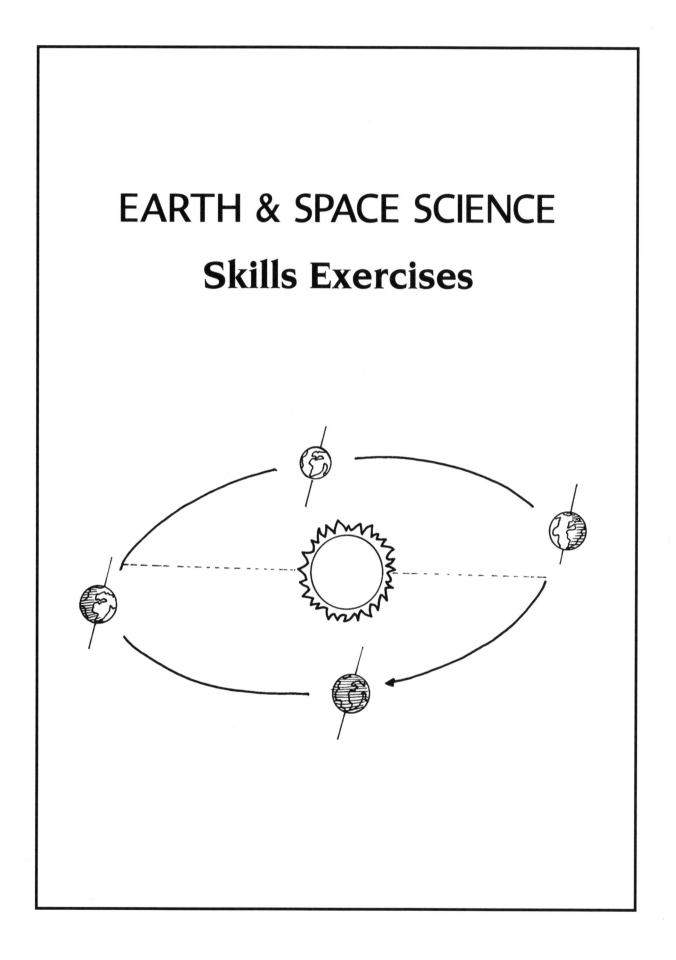

THE FAMOUS 10

The famous ten—the sun and nine planets—make up our solar system. But ten may not be the right number! Many scientists suspect that there's another planet out there. In any case, we know about nine of them. On the next page, you will make a rough design of the solar system. It will be "rough" because you can't really show the accurate orbits and distances for each planet on a small piece of paper. But you can show that you know where they are.

First, gather the information you need about the solar system by completing the chart below. Then get your markers or colored pencils and draw your own diagram of the solar system on page 11. Follow the directions at the bottom of page 11.

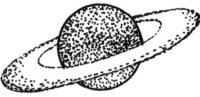

Number in Order from the Sun	PLANET	Number of Known Satellites	Colors, Features, Special Characteristics

Find these solar system facts, and then use them to help you with your design.

1. Johannes Kepler discovered that the paths planets follow are _____ in shape.

2. The point at which a planet is the greatest distance away from the sun in its orbit is called _____ .

3. The point at which the planet is closest to the sun in its orbit is called _____ .

4. The asteroid belt in our solar system is found between the planets _____ and _____ .

5. The inner planets are _____, _____, _____, and _____ .

6. The outer planets are _____, _____, _____, _____, and _____ .

Use with page 11.

Name _____

Use with page 10.

Draw the sun in the center of the box below. Add each planet in its orbit. Draw and color the planets to match their characteristics as best you can. Include the moons of each planet. Include the asteroid belt. Label the sun, the planets, and the asteroids.

Name

SOLAR SYSTEM SLEUTHING

Space has plenty of mysteries, even the space that we know best—our solar system. Floating around on this page are clues to mystery planets. Figure out which planet matches each clue, and write the code for that planet by the clue.

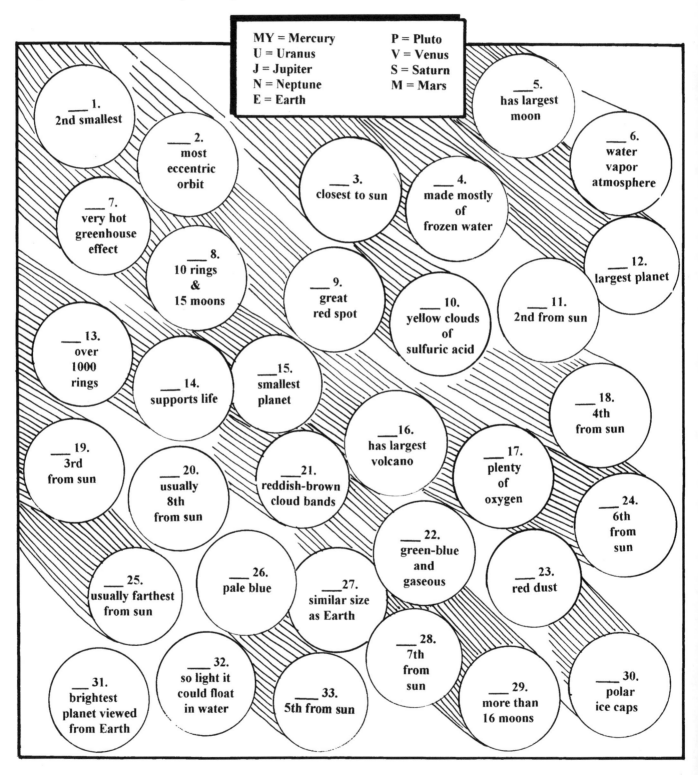

MY = Mercury   P = Pluto
U = Uranus   V = Venus
J = Jupiter   S = Saturn
N = Neptune   M = Mars
E = Earth

___1. 2nd smallest

___2. most eccentric orbit

___3. closest to sun

___4. made mostly of frozen water

___5. has largest moon

___6. water vapor atmosphere

___7. very hot greenhouse effect

___8. 10 rings & 15 moons

___9. great red spot

___10. yellow clouds of sulfuric acid

___11. 2nd from sun

___12. largest planet

___13. over 1000 rings

___14. supports life

___15. smallest planet

___16. has largest volcano

___17. plenty of oxygen

___18. 4th from sun

___19. 3rd from sun

___20. usually 8th from sun

___21. reddish-brown cloud bands

___22. green-blue and gaseous

___23. red dust

___24. 6th from sun

___25. usually farthest from sun

___26. pale blue

___27. similar size as Earth

___28. 7th from sun

___29. more than 16 moons

___30. polar ice caps

___31. brightest planet viewed from Earth

___32. so light it could float in water

___33. 5th from sun

Name _____

12

HOT SPOTS

These sky gazers are viewing some amazing stuff and swapping stories about what they're seeing. Read the description from each viewer and decide what he or she is watching. Choose the answers from the box at the bottom of the page.

"I see! (or think I see) . . .

_____ 1. "a mysterious, bright, starlike object in the galaxy core"

_____ 2. "Betelgeuse . . . a large star of high luminosity"

_____ 3. "dark spots on the sun where gas is cooler"

_____ 4. "clouds of dust and gas where stars are born"

_____ 5. "a hot, self-luminous sphere of gas"

_____ 6. "a neutron star that rotates rapidly and gives out a beam of radiation picked up as a pulse"

_____ 7. "the core of a star left after a supernova explosion"

_____ 8. "billions of stars held together by gravitational attraction"

_____ 9. "a specific pattern of stars"

_____ 10. "a star suddenly exploding with increasing brightness"

_____ 11. "the surface of the sun which emits the radiation we can see"

_____ 12. "2 stars orbiting a common center of gravity"

_____ 13. "a white dwarf which has stopped radiating energy"

_____ 14. "the brightest star in the sky"

_____ 15. "a star explosion which increases the star's luminosity to 1000 times that of a nova"

_____ 16. "a star that has collapsed after using its fuel"

white dwarf	Andromeda
red supergiant	black dwarf
Milky Way	variable star
quasar	solar flares
neutron star	chromosphere
black hole	Sirius A
binary star	nebulae
constellation	pulsar
galaxy	sunspots
nova	supernova
photosphere	star
corona	

_____ 17. "a star whose brightness changes"

_____ 18. "a nearby galaxy"

_____ 19. "our galaxy"

_____ 20. "very hot gas of the sun visible only during a total eclipse of the sun"

_____ 21. "sudden increases in brightness of the chromosphere of the sun"

_____ 22. "a collapsed star from which light cannot escape"

_____ 23. "bright red layer of sun surface containing hydrogen gas"

Name _____

CLOSE ENCOUNTERS

If you encountered a moving object in space, would you know what you've run into? (Or what has run into you?) Do you know the difference between a **comet** and a **coma**, an **asteroid** and a **meteoroid**, a **meteor** and a **meteorite**? For each of these descriptions, what is it that you've run into when you've encountered . . .

_____ 1. the solid portion of a comet?

_____ 2. a briefly visible meteor?

_____ 3. a meteor that strikes Earth's surface?

_____ 4. the largest asteroid ever found?

_____ 5. long streaks of bright light caused when a meteoroid gets close to the ground as it's burning up?

_____ 6. the large halo made of dust and gas that forms around the nucleus of a comet when it gets close to the sun?

_____ 7. a group of objects orbiting between Mars and Jupiter?

_____ 8. one of several heavenly bodies named for their discoverers?

_____ 9. a mass of frozen gases, cosmic dust, and rocky particles?

_____ 10. a meteoroid that has reached Earth's atmosphere?

_____ 11. fragments of matter similar in composition to planets that orbit the sun?

_____ 12. small fragments of matter (not asteroids) orbiting the sun?

_____ 13. a space curiosity that returns to Earth's view approximately every 76 years?

And, can you answer these?

_____ 14. What do comets orbit?

_____ 15. Where does a comet's tail point

_____ 16. What shape is a comet's path?

Name _____

COOL MOVES

Earth and its friends in the solar system make some fancy moves. And some of them are not even what they seem to your eyes! Because they watched the sun rise and set every day, people in ancient times thought the sun traveled across the sky or around Earth. They were wrong about this. In the last 500 years, scientists have learned a lot about the movements of Earth, moon, and other planets and bodies in space.

Describe each of these awesome moves or forces:

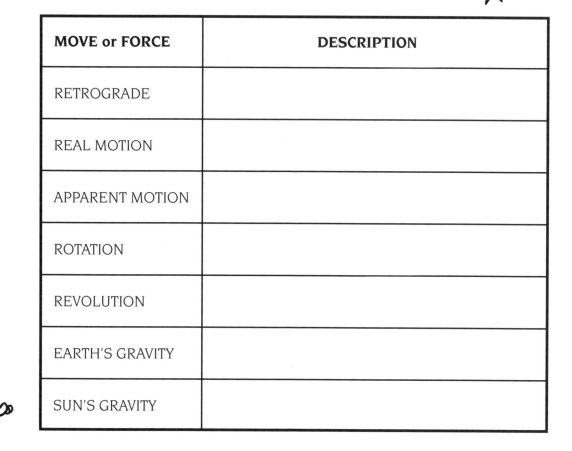

MOVE or FORCE	DESCRIPTION
RETROGRADE	
REAL MOTION	
APPARENT MOTION	
ROTATION	
REVOLUTION	
EARTH'S GRAVITY	
SUN'S GRAVITY	

Answer these questions about Earth's cool moves:

1. What is caused by Earth's rotation? _____

2. How long does it take for Earth to rotate once? _____

3. Who discovered that things did not revolve around Earth? _____

4. What are Earth's two **real** motions? _____ and _____

5. What is caused by Earth's revolution around the sun? _____

6. How long does it take for one revolution? _____

Name _____

REASONS FOR SEASONS

What's with the seasons? How do they know when to come and go? It all has to do with the movements of Earth in relation to the sun. Here are some reasons. You fill in the blanks to tell what the reason explains.

1. **Reason** for _____:
Because Earth is tilted 23½° from a line perpendicular to its orbit, the length of daylight varies and because of the angle at which the sun's energy strikes a given location through the year.

2. **Reason** for _____ in the Northern Hemisphere:
Because the Northern Hemisphere is tilted toward the sun for a few months.

3. **Reason** for _____ in the Northern Hemisphere and _____ in the
Southern Hemisphere: Because Earth's tilt is sideways to the sun, and hours of daylight and darkness are the same in both hemispheres on about September 22.

4. **Reason** for _____ in the Northern Hemisphere:
Because the North Pole is tilted almost directly toward the sun on about June 21.

5. **Reason** for _____ in the Southern Hemisphere:
Because the South Pole is tilted away from the sun on about June 21.

6. **Reason** for _____ in the Southern Hemisphere:
Because the Southern Hemisphere is tilted toward the sun for a few months.

7. **Reason** for _____ in the Northern Hemisphere:
Because the South Pole is tilted almost directly toward the sun on about December 21.

8. **Reason** for _____ in the Northern Hemisphere and _____ in the Southern
Hemisphere: Because Earth's tilt is sideways to the sun and hours of daylight and darkness are the same in both hemispheres on about March 20.

9. **Reason** for _____ in the Southern Hemisphere:
Because the South Pole is tilted almost directly toward the sun on about December 21.

10. **Reason** for _____ hours of daylight at the South Pole: Because the South Pole is tilted directly toward the sun on about December 21.

On the diagram at the right, label winter solstice, summer solstice, fall equinox, and spring equinox for the Northern Hemisphere.

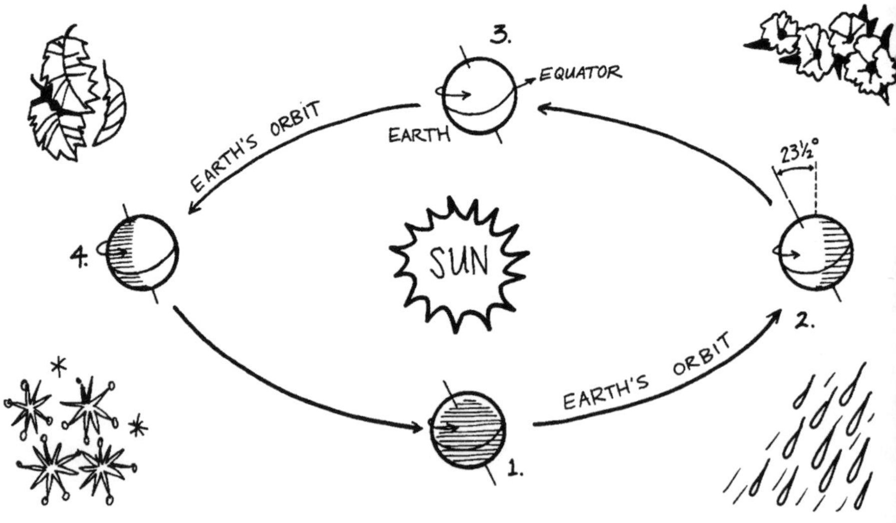

Name _____

MOON TALK

Wax, wane, crescent, gibbous, quarter, full, revolve, rotate, lunar . . . are words you need to know if you're going to speak **moon**. These describe the movements and phases of the moon. Antonia Astronaut, who incidentally is on a moon walk, is telling you some things about the moon. Match each label in the box (A-H) with the correct phase or position of the moon in the diagram. Then match the same labels with Antonia's descriptions below. Write the correct letter on the line.

A. first quarter   C. full moon   E. waxing crescent   G. waning gibbous
B. third quarter   D. new moon   F. waxing gibbous   H. waning crescent

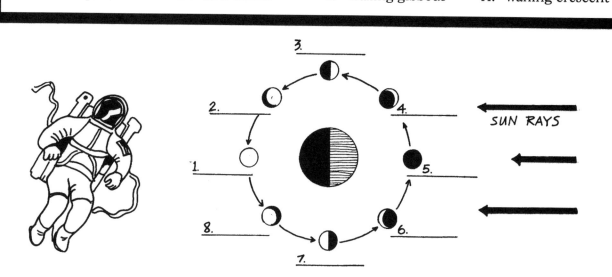

_____ 9. "The moon lies between the sun and Earth so the side of the moon facing Earth is dark and the moon is not visible."

_____ 10. "More than a quarter of the moon is visible, and the visible portion is becoming smaller as the moon moves toward the third quarter phase."

_____ 11. "The moon has moved eastward in its orbit from the new moon phase and forms a 90° angle with the sun and Earth, and the moon appears half bright and half dark."

_____ 12. "Although less than a quarter of the moon is visible now, the visible portion is getting larger as the moon moves from the new moon phase toward the first quarter phase."

_____ 13. "The moon is aligned with the sun and Earth, Earth being in the middle. The entire side of the moon facing Earth is bright and visible."

_____ 14. "Less than a quarter of the moon is visible, and the visible part is getting even smaller as the moon moves toward the new moon phase."

_____ 15. "The moon is moving toward the full moon phase, and presently more than a quarter of it is visible on Earth."

_____ 16. "The moon, sun, and Earth are forming a 90° angle, so the side of the moon facing Earth is half dark and half bright. The visible part of the moon will be getting smaller as it moves toward the new moon phase."

Name _____

CASTING SHADOWS

Have you ever seen the sun disappear? Or watched an eerie shadow move across the moon? Imagine what it was like for primitive people when the sky suddenly fell dark in the middle of the day! When three celestial objects fall into alignment, some great shadows are the result. These shadows are called eclipses of the moon or sun, and they're pretty spectacular to watch! These eclipse-watchers have written down some information about eclipses. Do they have all their facts straight? Write T (true) or F (false) next to each statement.

_____ 1. A solar eclipse occurs when Earth falls between the sun and the moon.

_____ 2. All eclipses are visible.

_____ 3. All eclipses are total.

_____ 4. The umbra is the inner part of the shadow.

_____ 5. Eclipses of the sun occur 2–4 times a year.

_____ 6. A lunar eclipse occurs when the moon travels through the shadow of Earth.

_____ 7. There are about 2 lunar eclipses a year.

_____ 8. A lunar eclipse can take place only when the moon is full.

_____ 9. A total solar eclipse lasts a few minutes.

_____ 10. In a solar eclipse, no sunlight penetrates the umbra.

_____ 11. A total lunar eclipse occurs when the moon passes through Earth's penumbra.

_____ 12. Partial lunar eclipses occur more often than total eclipses.

_____ 13. A solar eclipse may last over 3 hours.

_____ 14. A total solar eclipse is visible at all spots on Earth.

_____ 15. All lunar eclipses are total.

_____ 16. In a total solar eclipse, the moon completely covers the sun.

_____ 17. Lunar eclipses occur every 3 years.

_____ 18. A lunar eclipse may last over 3 hours.

_____ 19. The penumbra is the outer part of the shadow.

_____ 20. When the sun's disk is covered in an eclipse, the corona is still visible.

Label the diagrams below **solar eclipse** or **lunar eclipse**.
Label **Earth, moon, umbra,** and **penumbra** on each diagram.

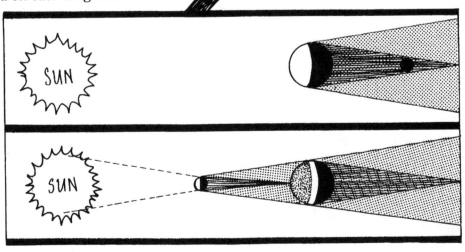

Name _____

WHAT'S OUT THERE?

For many years, human beings have been snooping around in space, trying to find out what's out there. They've done their snooping using many different methods, instruments, and contraptions. This puzzle is hiding the names of several tools they've used in their quest for information about space. Use the clues to find the answers for each tool. If the answers are right, the letters in the squares will spell the name of a mystery spaceship that has a famous history (# = space between words).

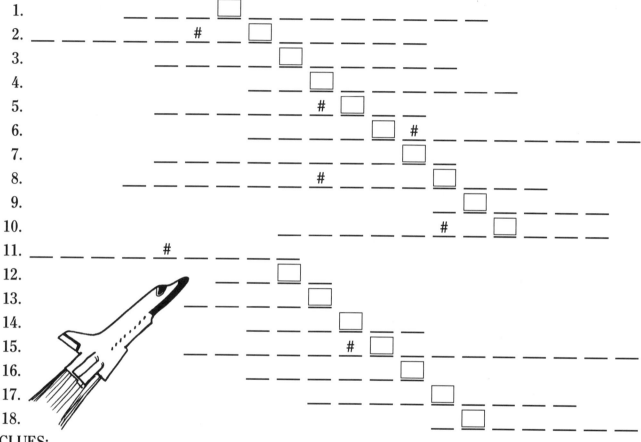

CLUES:

1. an instrument that separates light into various wavelengths
2. a reusable craft for transporting people and supplies to and from space
3. telescope that uses an objective lens to bend light toward the plane where the image is formed
4. instrument that makes small, distant objects visible
5. a workshop in space where astronauts can carry out experiments
6. living and working quarters for astronauts in space
7. telescope that collects light with a mirror
8. U.S. space program that put astronauts on the moon
9. U.S. space project that gave astronauts practice piloting spacecraft and working in space
10. rocket-launched vehicle that carries equipment for gathering data above Earth's atmosphere
11. astronaut Neil Armstrong took one of these on July 16, 1969
12. agency that oversees the U.S. space program
13. instrument that photographs light wavelengths to find movements of space objects (spectro _____)
14. force produced by expansions of gases that pushes a rocket forward
15. reflector disk that collects radio waves
16. action-reaction engines that propel an object forward
17. an object that revolves around another object
18. U.S. space project that gathered data on the basics of space flight

Mystery Spaceship __ __ __ __ __ __ __ __ __ __ __ __ __ __ __ __ __ __
1   2   3   4   5   6   7   8   9   10   12   13   14   15   16   17   18

Name _____

SPACE VENTURES

Although people dreamed of venturing into outer space for many years, it was not until the second half of the nineteenth century that anyone actually traveled into space. Some of the most notable discoveries and ventures in space exploration are described below, out of the order in which they occurred. Do some research in your science book, encyclopedia, almanac, or other reference books to find the year that each of these space ventures took place. Then place these ventures on to the timeline on page 21. Add your own space drawings to the timeline, too!

_____ 1. **Mariner 9** (U.S.) 1st craft to orbit another planet (Mars)

_____ 2. **Explorer I** (1st U.S. satellite) in orbit

_____ 3. **Ranger 7** (U.S.) first close-range photos of the moon

_____ 4. **Hubble Space Telescope** launched

_____ 5. **Mariner 10** (U.S.) flies past Venus to get a look at Mercury

_____ 6. **Salyut 7** Soviet cosmonauts set a record for 237 days in space

_____ 7. **Gemini 6 and 7** U.S. astronauts complete 1st space rendezvous

_____ 8. **Tsiolkovsky**, Russian scientist, publishes first proof that space travel is possible

_____ 9. **Challenger**, U.S. space shuttle, explodes soon after take-off

_____ 10. **Luna 1** (USSR) first space craft to orbit the sun

_____ 11. **Luna 2, 3** (USSR) first spacecraft to orbit and photograph the moon

_____ 12. **Viking** (U.S.) photographs and gets soil samples form Mars

_____ 13. **Columbia** (U.S. shuttle) takes 1st congressman, Bill Nelson, into space

_____ 14. **Pioneer 11** (U.S.) travels to Jupiter and Saturn

_____ 15. U.S. space program resumes after **Challenger** tragedy

_____ 16. **Trios 1** (U.S.) 1st successful weather satellite

_____ 17. Physicist **Robert Goddard** launches 1st successful liquid fuel rocket

_____ 18. **Mariner 2** (U.S.) 1st spacecraft to a planet (Venus)

_____ 19. **Luna 9** (USSR) 1st landing on moon

_____ 20. **Alan Shepard**, 1st U.S. astronaut in space

_____ 21. **Zond 5** (USSR) 1st circumlunar flight

_____ 22. **Apollo 8** 1st U.S. craft to orbit moon

_____ 23. U.S. launches **Skylab Space Station**

_____ 24. 1st space walk, Soviet **Alexi Leonov**

_____ 25. **Voyagers 1, 2** (U.S. crafts), leave for Jupiter, Saturn, Uranus, and Neptune

_____ 26. **Sally Ride** 1st U.S. woman in space

_____ 27. **Shannon Lucid** sets U.S. record for longest stay in space

_____ 28. **Sputnik** (USSR) 1st man-made object to orbit Earth

_____ 29. Soviet **Uri A. Gagarin**, 1st man in space

_____ 30. **Apollo 11** (U.S.) 1st astronauts to land on moon, Neil Armstrong and Edwin Aldrin

_____ 31. 1st flight of space shuttle **Columbia**

_____ 32. **Sputnik 2** (USSR) carries a dog, 1st living thing into space

_____ 33. **Friendship 7** carries 1st American, John Glenn, into orbit

_____ 34. 1st woman in space, Soviet **Valentina Tereshkova**, orbits Earth

_____ 35. **Gemini 4** Edward H. White I is 1st American to walk in space

_____ 36. **Surveyor 1** 1st U.S. spacecraft to soft-land on the moon

_____ 37. **Apollo 13** aborts moon mission due to damaged engine; astronauts returned safely to Earth

_____ 38. **Luna 10** (USSR) 1st spacecraft to orbit moon

Use with page 21.

Name _____

Use with page 20.

SPACE EXPLORATION TIMELINE

Write the key word of each venture from page 20 into the correct date box on the timeline. Some years will have more than one answer.

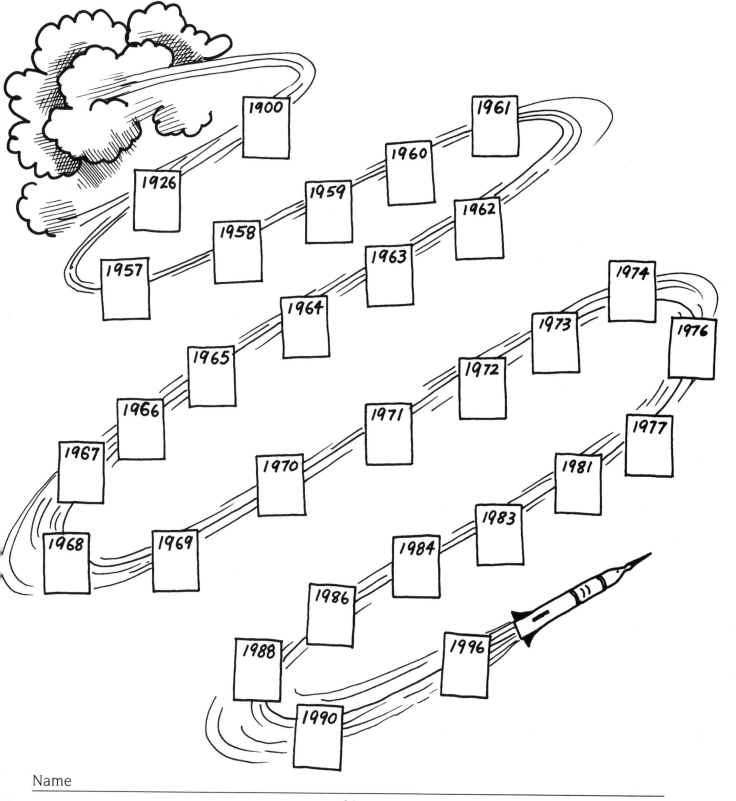

Name

THE AIR UP THERE

Zak and Zeke want to explore Earth's atmosphere. They think their amazing balloon can take them high enough to learn all about the atmosphere. Are they right? Here are some things they'll need to learn before they get too far.

1. Label the layers of the atmosphere: troposphere, thermosphere, stratosphere, mesosphere.
2. Also label: **tropopause, exosphere, ionosphere.**
3. Tell what layer or feature is described in each phrase below. Write **TR** for **troposphere**, **TH** for **thermosphere**, **M** for **mesosphere**, **S** for **stratosphere**, **I** for **ionosphere**, **EX** for **exosphere**, and **TPP** for **tropopause**.

_____ a. contains dust, water vapor, and 75% of all gases
_____ b. extends from 10–20 km above Earth
_____ c. layer with coldest temperatures: –100° C
_____ d. layer extends 85 km above Earth into space
_____ e. temperature decreases with increasing height
_____ f. the ozone layer is in this layer
_____ g. contains the Van Allen Belts of radiation
_____ h. layer where all weather occurs
_____ i. ceiling to the weather zone
_____ j. extends from 15 or 20 km to 50 km above Earth
_____ k. temperatures increase in this layer
_____ l. begins at about 500 km above Earth
_____ m. top portion of troposphere
_____ n. layer has 2 parts
_____ o. lower part has temperatures –50°C; upper temperatures are 0° C
_____ p. jet streams are just below this
_____ q. extends 50–85 km above Earth's surface
_____ r. filled with electronically charged particles

4. What is in the air that makes up Earth's atmosphere? _____

_____

5. What is so important about ozone? _____

_____

6. What is atmospheric pressure? _____

_____

7. Why does air pressure vary? _____

_____

8. Will Zak & Zeke get above the troposphere? _____

Name _____

AIR ON THE MOVE

Amelia Dareheart's plane keeps getting caught in various forms of moving air. For each description, fill in the name of the predicament in which she finds herself. Use the labels in the box to help you with your task.

doldrums

cyclone

jet stream

hurricane

prevailing westerlies

water spout

front

blizzard

tornado

land breeze

polar easterlies

sea breeze

gale

trade winds

_____ 1. She's caught in a wind that blows toward the equator from about 30° N and 30° S of the equator. What is it?

_____ 2. Ahhhh—relief! She's flying in wind-less _____ along the equator!

_____ 3. Warm air moving toward the poles between 30°–60° latitude in the Northern Hemisphere is pushing her along at a good speed. She's in a _____ .

_____ 4. She's spinning out of control in a low-pressure system where air is whirling counterclockwise toward the center of a _____ .

_____ 5. Warm air over land rises and cool air from the water is moving in, pulling her along in air moving from sea to land. This is a _____ .

_____ 6. Between the North Pole and 60° latitude, she's buzzing along in cold, dry, dense, horizontal air currents called _____ .

_____ 7. She's caught in the eye of a storm with warm, moist air rotating around her. She's flying in a _____ . Bad idea!

_____ 8. Now she's in a body of air that got its properties from the place it formed. It is called a _____ .

_____ 9. Moving along quickly, she's in the _____ , the narrow belt of wind near the tropopause that formed when warm tropical air met cold polar air.

_____ 10. Watch out for that _____ , a large mass of moving air.

_____ 11. It's nighttime, and the warm air over the water rises and is replaced by cooler air from the land. This moves her along with the _____ .

_____ 12. She's twisting in hot air spinning upwards; she's caught in the center of a _____ .

_____ 13. This time she's over the sea, in a funnel of water called a _____ .

_____ 14. Oh Amelia! Now it's snow whipped by heavy wind, called a _____ .

Name

WEATHER OR NOT

All the weather forecasters in the town of Secret have this annoying habit of telling about the weather without telling exactly what it is! See if you can give the correct term for the weather condition or event that they describe.

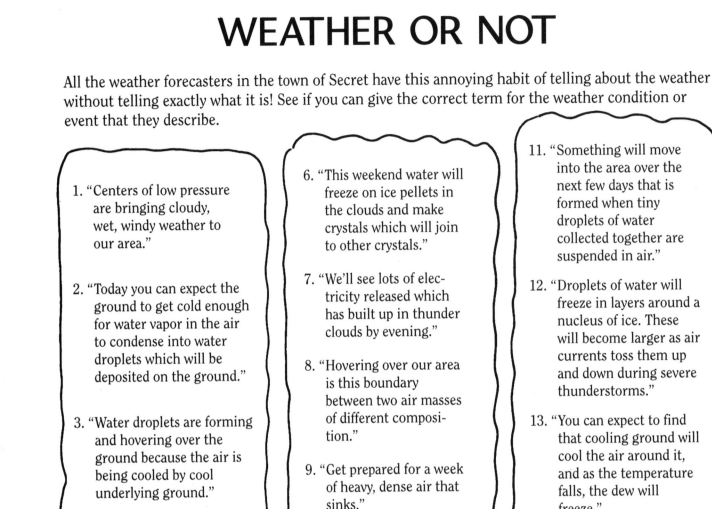

1. "Centers of low pressure are bringing cloudy, wet, windy weather to our area."

2. "Today you can expect the ground to get cold enough for water vapor in the air to condense into water droplets which will be deposited on the ground."

3. "Water droplets are forming and hovering over the ground because the air is being cooled by cool underlying ground."

4. "Whirling funnels of air are expected to form between the bottom of a storm cloud and the ground."

5. "I predict we'll see tiny water droplets in the clouds join together to make drops before the day is over."

6. "This weekend water will freeze on ice pellets in the clouds and make crystals which will join to other crystals."

7. "We'll see lots of electricity released which has built up in thunder clouds by evening."

8. "Hovering over our area is this boundary between two air masses of different composition."

9. "Get prepared for a week of heavy, dense air that sinks."

10. "Centers of high pressure will bring dry, sunny, settled weather for the next several days."

11. "Something will move into the area over the next few days that is formed when tiny droplets of water collected together are suspended in air."

12. "Droplets of water will freeze in layers around a nucleus of ice. These will become larger as air currents toss them up and down during severe thunderstorms."

13. "You can expect to find that cooling ground will cool the air around it, and as the temperature falls, the dew will freeze."

14. "Residents will need to evacuate due to a storm with extremely high winds developing over the warm tropical ocean offshore."

15. "This afternoon, air will expand several times at great speeds and cause booming sounds."

RAIN   LOWS

FOG   CLOUDS

FRONTS

KSNO

THUNDER   SNOW

DEW   TORNADO

FROST

HURRICANE

LIGHTNING

COLD AIR

W-WET

HAIL

HIGHS

K-HOT

Use with page 25.

Name

Use with page 24.   WARM FRONT   DROUGHT   TORNADO WARNING   ANTICYCLONE

SLEET # MORE WEATHER OR NOT

DEW POINT   BLIZZARD   CYCLONES

PRECIPITATION

16. "The weather tonight will be dominated by air movement that is caused by air moving from areas of high to low pressure."

17. "You can expect sunlight to shine through rain drops and break up into its many colors."

18. "You can expect some water to fall from the sky in the form of rain, hail, sleet, or snow."

19. "We'll be surrounded for a few days with lighter air that rises."

20. "The measure of the amount of water vapor in the air will be low for the rest of the week."

21. "I'll be right back to report the temperature at which condensation will occur today."

22. "The warm front we had yesterday has stopped moving. It is likely to remain in place for several days."

23. "We're looking here at an area of high pressure where the air is circulating clockwise and causing areas of fair weather."

24. "We're notifying the county that severe tornado conditions exist."

25. "The temperature of the air, rather than getting cooler at higher altitudes, is warmer, and this air is holding the cold air down near the ground, causing fog in the valleys."

26. "Air is flowing out counterclockwise from an area of low pressure and causing a major storm."

27. "We're notifying the county that tornado conditions could develop."

28. "Right now raindrops are falling out there through a layer of air that is less than –3° C. This is causing these drops to freeze."

29. "Get ready for a weekend of high winds and heavy, blowing snow."

30. "The whole Midwest is experiencing a prolonged period without rain or any other precipitation."

31. "This weekend, a cold air mass will invade a warm air mass, bringing rain showers and thunderstorms, followed by cooler temperatures."

32. "Next week, you can expect this warm air mass to meet this cold air mass over the southern part of the state and bring rain and snow."

ND   RAINBOWS   STATIONARY FRONT

TORNADO WATCH   RELATIVE HUMIDITY

TEMPERATURE INVERSION

WARM AIR   COLD FRONT

K-DRY   W-KOOL   W-SMOG

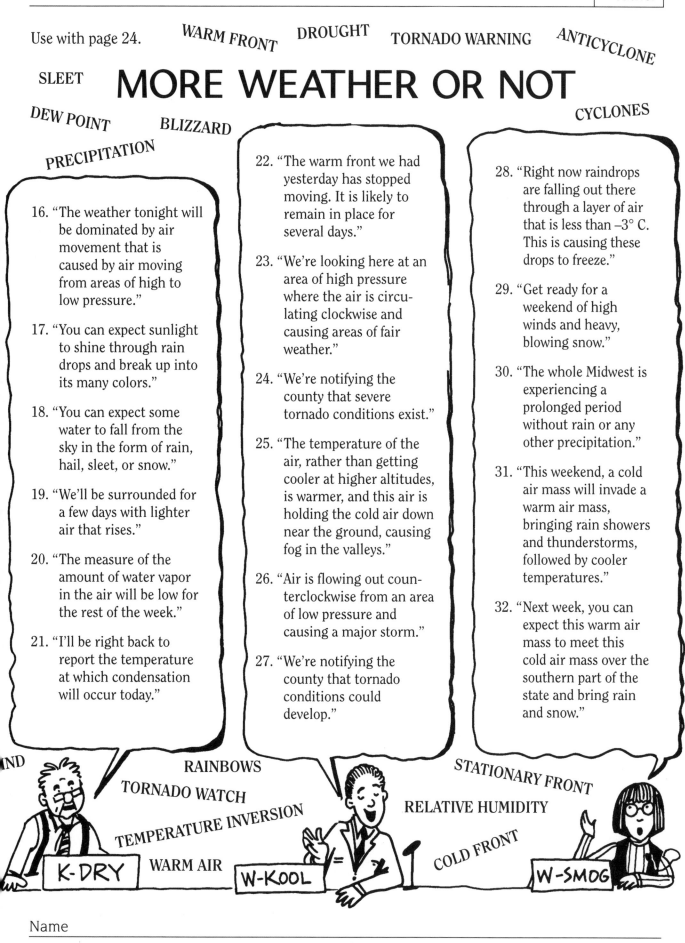

Name

UP FRONT

Where is the front of the front? And does a front have a back, or just a front? What do you know about the fronts that are so dominant in forming the weather around you? See if you can tell one front from another.

  I. Fill in all the blanks to show that you understand the characteristics of each type of front.

  II. Then label each drawing correctly: **warm front, cold front, stationary front,** or **occluded front.**

A **warm front** develops when a _____ air mass meets a _____ air mass. The _____ air is less _____ than the _____ air and slides up over it. One of the first signs of a warm front is _____ clouds. _____ clouds form as the front continues to move. _____ clouds may develop and produce precipitation in the form of _____ or _____ .

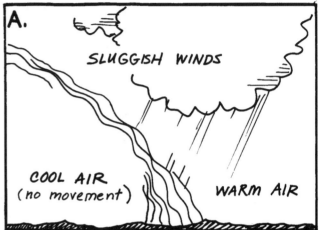

A **cold front** develops when a _____ air mass invades a _____ air mass. The _____ air forces the _____ air rapidly upward along a steep incline. The kinds of clouds that tend to form along a cold front are _____ and _____ . These produce _____ . The passage of a cold front brings _____ temperatures and _____ weather.

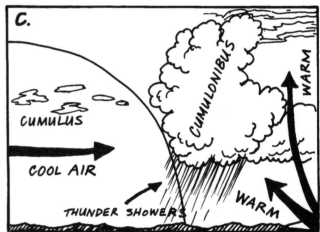

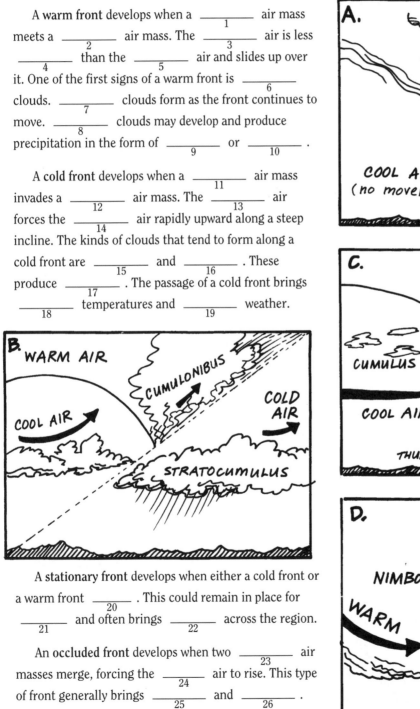

A **stationary front** develops when either a cold front or a warm front _____ . This could remain in place for _____ and often brings _____ across the region.

An **occluded front** develops when two _____ air masses merge, forcing the _____ air to rise. This type of front generally brings _____ and _____ .

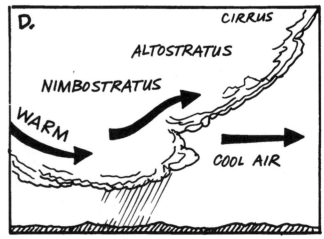

WHAT DIFFERENCE DOES IT MAKE?

Of course you know that climate is the average long-range weather of a place. You probably also know that different areas of the world have different climate conditions. This means differences in temperature, amounts of rain or snow, humidity, or cloudiness. But . . . do you know why? Brush up on climate causes by finding out how each of these factors affects climate conditions. Write phrases or sentences to explain the effects of each one on climate.

latitude	Earth's revolution around the sun
tilt of Earth	bodies of water
ocean currents	altitude (elevation)
topography	large land masses
prevailing winds	large, permanent ice surfaces
cultural factors such as cities	

Name

CLIMATE CHOICES

People often choose to visit or live in a place because of the climate—the long-range weather conditions in a region. Sometimes people want to vacation in a climate where they wouldn't want to live all the time. Do you live in a place that has a climate you're crazy about?

The chart on page 29 describes different climate types of the world. Read these carefully to review the features of certain climatic regions. Then answer these questions about climatic regions for living, working, or vacationing. You will need a good world map or atlas to help you.

1. Oksana and her friends are looking for a vacation spot for good skiing in June or July. What climate type should they visit? _____

2. Sorena and Gregory are scientists heading for some work in the Kalahari Desert of southern Africa in January. What climate conditions can they expect? _____

3. The Swiss Hiking Club is looking for a place in North America for 2 weeks of hiking in August. They want to be in coniferous forests with moderate summer temperatures. What climate zone should they head for? _____

4. The Chiang family wants to move to a place where there is very little moisture and hot temperatures most of the year. What climate type(s) or types would be good choices(s)?

_____

5. Melissa lives in northern California, where there is a good bit of moisture during the winter, especially next to the mountains. The temperatures are mild—around 40°–50°. What kind of climate is this? _____

6. Spending the summer on a ranch in the Great Plains of central Montana, Jake is surprised at how hot the temperatures are and how little rain there is. What climate type is he in? _____

7. Would the west coast of southern California be a good place to live for Lahaina, who has bad asthma and needs a place that is very warm and dry all year? _____

8. Jason chose to visit Death Valley, an inland desert in California where summers are hot with temperatures higher than 100° and less than 5 inches of rain a year. What climate type did he choose to experience? _____

9. Explorers in the Amazon River Basin in South America get a rain shower every afternoon in a climate that is warm and humid all year. What climate zone are they visiting? _____

10. Are college kids who spend their spring break on the beaches near Miami, Florida, choosing to be in a humid subtropical climate? _____

11. Tourists fortunate enough to afford a safari on the great savanna of Africa to view the huge animals which roam in Kenya enjoy a month of dry, warm temperatures during the long, dry winter season. What climate have they chosen?

_____

12. The Malcovech family chose to visit Alaska in July. They found cool temperatures, little precipitation, and nighttime frosts. They also found dense, coniferous forests and permafrost underfoot. What climate are they enjoying? _____

13. If you wish to farm in an area of tall prairie grasses and year-round precipitation, would you choose a humid continental climate or a temperate marine climate? _____

14. The Johnsons want to live where there are 4 different seasons. They want snow in winter and long, warm, dry summers. Should they choose a subarctic taiga climate? _____

Use with page 29.

Name _____

Use with page 28.

CLIMATE TYPES

All temperatures are Fahrenheit.

CLIMATE	CHARACTERISTICS
WET TROPICAL	low latitudes: 10° N & S of equator • warm all year • no winter • heavy precipitation: 80+ in. a year • high humidity • thundershowers most days • average temp 80° and higher • dense vegetation • rainforest, jungle, swamps
HUMID CONTINENTAL CYCLONIC	5°–70° latitude • long, warm summers at lower latitudes • long, cold winters toward poles (far below 0° in winter) • year-round rain and snow • most precipitation in summer • 25–60 in. of precipitation • tall grasses and forests (coniferous & deciduous)
WET-DRY TROPICAL	10°–20° latitude • tall grasses and scattered trees • less precipitation than wet tropics • high temperatures—in 90s • rainy summer season • long dry winter season
SUBARCTIC CYCLONIC (Taiga)	50°–70° latitude • short, cool summers • bitterly cold winters • temperature range: – 0° to 100° • less than 20 in. precipitation, mostly from summer rain • frozen subsoil (permafrost) • coniferous forests (taiga)
DRY TROPICAL and SEMI-ARID TROPICAL	15°–30° latitude • semi-arid or arid steppes or desert • annual precipitation less than 30 in. on steppe; less than 10 in. on desert • average temperatures in 90s • Desert highs are over 130° • short grasses; desert shrubs • long, dry season
DRY CONTINENTAL CYCLONIC	35°–50° latitude on lee side of mountains or far inland on large continents • hot summers; over 100° • low precipitation 5–20 in. • mid-latitude steppes & deserts
DRY SUBTROPICAL	20°–40° latitude • semi-arid but cooler than tropical • annual precipitation under 15 in. • long, dry season • summer—top temperatures 110° • winter—sometimes below freezing
TEMPERATE MARINE CYCLONIC	40°–60 ° latitude on west coasts of continents • temperatures moderated by westerly winds • mild winters; average 40° • mild summers; under 85° • 20–30 in. of precipitation • year-round precipitation
MEDITERRANEAN DRY-SUMMER SUBTROPICAL	30°–40° latitude on west-facing coasts • warm, dry summers • mild, wet winters • 15–40 in. of precipitation a year
POLAR (Tundra)	beyond Arctic/Antarctic Circle • long, cold winters • no real summer • up to -70° • high temperatures below 60° • less than 15 in. precipitation • permafrost; no trees • polar ice cap in many places
HUMID SUBTROPICAL	25°–35° latitude on east side of continents • influenced by warm, ocean air • moderate precipitation all year • 30–60 in. a year precipitation • short, mild winters • occasionally below freezing • 80s—average summer temperatures
HIGHLAND	at many latitudes • cooler than lower altitudes at same latitude • great temperature range between day and night • generally humid • more precipitation on lower, windward slopes • permanent snow at high elevations

Name

OCEAN MOTIONS

Currents and tides . . . rolling waves and breakers . . . upwellings and tsunamis. The ocean never stops moving—that one thing is for sure! There are constant motions on the ocean. Some of them you want to be in. Some you want to watch. Others you want to hide from.
Define each of these motions. Write your definitions on the back of this page.

A. surface current   **B. density current**   **C. waves**   **D. tides**
E. upwellings   **F. tsunami**   **G. surf**

Answer these questions or complete these statements about ocean motions.

1. Upwellings bring _____ to the surface of the ocean.

2. Surface currents are caused by _____.

3. What ocean movements are affected by the moon's gravity? _____

4. What direction do most surface currents north of the equator move? _____

5. What direction do most surface currents south of the equator move? _____

6. How do cold currents affect climate? _____

7. How do warm currents affect climate? _____

8. What causes circulation in deep water? _____

9. What two things affect the density of water? _____ and _____

10. Does evaporation of salt water cause density to (increase) or (decrease)? _____

11. Another name for a thermohaline current is _____.

12. Is very salty water more or less dense than less salty water? _____

13. Is cold ocean water more or less dense than warmer water? _____

14. Does polar water diluted by melting ice become more or less dense? _____

15. Does heavy rainfall make ocean water more or less dense? _____

16. Which ocean motion is caused by earthquakes? _____

17. Which ocean motion occurs when a wave strikes the bottom of the ocean? _____

Name _____

CATCH A WAVE

These surfers and swimmers are having a great time catching and riding waves. Show how well you know waves by answering the questions about which surfer or swimmer is where.

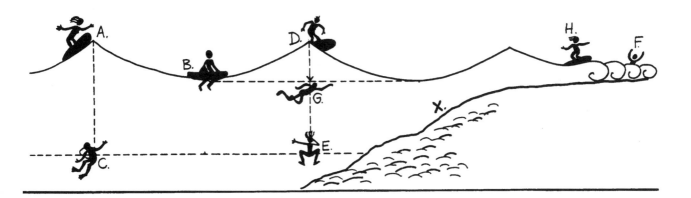

1. Which surfers are on the crests of waves? _____

2. Which surfers/swimmers are in deep-water waves? _____

3. Which surfers/swimmers are in shallow-water waves? _____

4. Where is surfer B? _____

5. The distance between surfers A and D is called the _____.

6. Which swimmers are at the wave base? _____

7. Which surfers/swimmers are in the surf or breakers? _____

8. The distance between which 2 surfers/swimmers is equal to the wave height? _____

9. The time it takes the waves A and B to pass any point is called the _____.

10. The distance between surfer A and swimmer C is equal to ½ the _____.

11. What is a wave, anyway? _____

12. How do particles of water in a wave move?_____

13. What happens when a deep-water wave strikes the bottom of the ocean? _____

    _____

14. What kind of a wave is caused by seismic activity? _____.

15. A wave moving in water that is deeper than ½ its wavelength is called a _____.

Name _____

WHICH TIDE IS WHICH?

Isaac Newton discovered that everything in the universe exerts a pull on everything else. So what does this have to do with ocean water? Well, the sun and moon are both large enough and close enough to Earth that their gravitational forces pull ocean water into a bulge. This causes tides.

But . . . different locations of the sun, moon, and Earth in relationship to each other result in different kinds of tides. Show the sharpness of your TIDE IQ by telling which tide is which in the diagrams below.

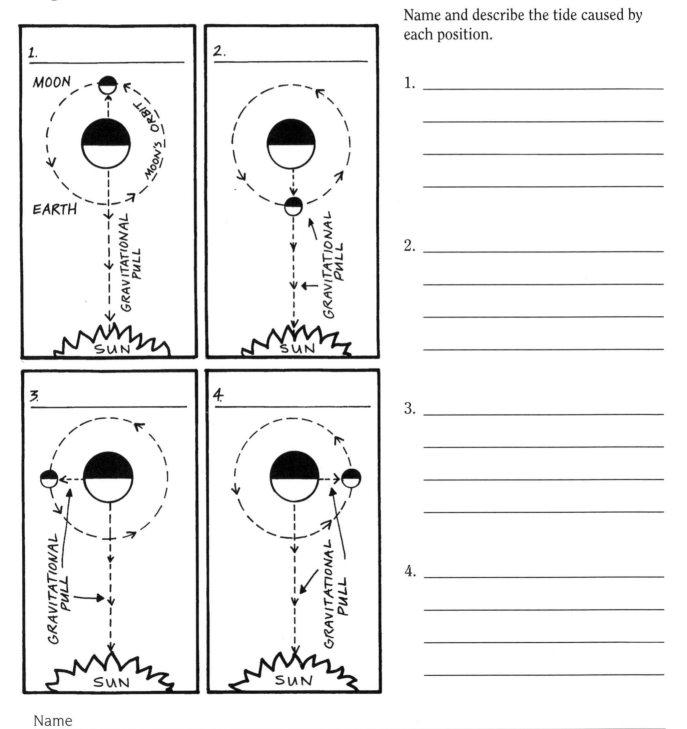

Name and describe the tide caused by each position.

1. _____

_____

_____

_____

2. _____

_____

_____

_____

_____

3. _____

_____

_____

_____

4. _____

_____

_____

_____

_____

Name _____

TIDE TALK

If the tide is out, is this a good place to set up your beach blanket? See if you know enough about tides to solve the puzzle. After you finish all the circles, the vertical word will answer the problem at the bottom of the page.

1. ○ — — — —
2. — ○ — — —
3. — — ○ — —
4. — — ○ — —
5. — — — ○ — — — —
6. — — ○ — —
7. — — — — ○ — —
8. — — — — ○ — —
9. — — — ○ — —
10. — ○ — — —
11. — — — — — — — — —
12. — — ○ — — — —
13. ○ — — —
14. — — — ○ — —
15. — — — ○ — —
16. — ○ — —

The area between the bulges of water is ——1——. Neap tides occur when the sun, moon, and Earth form a right ——2——. A rotational force of Earth-moon system causes a ——3—— in the ocean on the opposite side of Earth from the moon. Neap tides occur during the ——4—— and ——9—— quarter moon positions. The difference between the highest and lowest tides is the ——5——. Spring tides occur when the sun, moon, and Earth ——6——. These occur when high tides are highest and low tides are lowest: ——7——. Bulges of water in the ocean are ——8——. During neap tides, tidal range is at its ——10——. Two high and two low tides a day: ——11——. Minimum tides are ——12——. Spring tides occur when the moon is in a ——13—— or ——16—— position. One high and one low tide a day: ——14——. Spring tides occur ——15—— a month.

Vertical: Bulge of the ocean is pulled toward the moon by this.

Name

UPS & DOWNS AT THE BOTTOM

Most people never see much of the ocean floor. But if you did get a good look at it, you'd see that it's not just a flat, bland floor. The ocean floor has a topography like the dry surface of Earth—with mountains and valleys and plains. But the features of the underwater surface are even more spectacular and pronounced than the ones above water.

These are some topographical features of the ocean floor. Write the letter (A-G) that gives the correct description for each one. Then find the letter on the diagram below (S-Z) that shows an example of the feature.

FEATURE	DEFINITION	EXAMPLE
1. continental shelf	_____	_____
2. continental slope	_____	_____
3. abyssal plain	_____	_____
4. mid-ocean range	_____	_____
5. oceanic trench	_____	_____
6. seamount	_____	_____
7. island	_____	_____

A. steeply sloping edge of continental shelf that drops to the ocean basin

B. volcano that does not rise above sea level

C. mountain that rises above sea level

D. relatively flat part of continent covered by sea water

E. deep ocean trough

F. flat, almost level, area of ocean basin

G. underwater mountain chain

Name _____

DISAPPEARING ACT

Four agents are responsible for a powerful earthwide act that changes or carries away parts of earth's materials—even tough ones like mountains. These are the agents of weathering or erosion.

Name these agents:

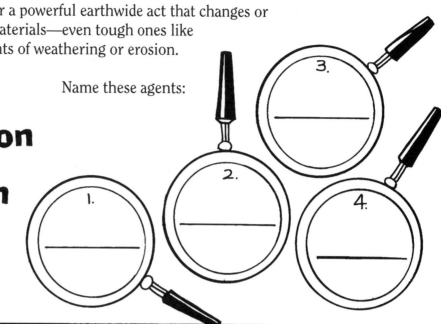

decomposition
disintegration
loess
talus
abrasion
deflation
weathering
oasis
creep
landslides
erosion
mudflows
slump
dune
rockfalls
gravity

Use the clues below to find out which processes and results these agents are using to do their disappearing acts.

CLUES

1. physical weathering; breakup of rocks into fragments
2. force that pulls material down a slope
3. process by which weathered materials are carried away
4. fertile green area in desert where winds have eroded land to a depth where water is present
5. material that accumulates at the bottom of a steep slope
6. blowing sand dropped by wind when an obstacle is met
7. windblown deposit of fine dust
8. rapid downslope movements of debris and dirt mixed with rain
9. loose material in layers slipping down a slope
10. scouring action of particles carried by wind
11. rapid movement of large amounts of material downslope
12. large masses of fallen rock
13. removal of loose material by wind
14. rocks formed from new substances
15. changes that rocks undergo near Earth's surface
16. slow downslope movements of materials

Name _____

WATER ON THE MOVE

Moving water is Earth's major agent of erosion—responsible for some of the most spectacular changes and landforms on the surface of Earth.

Here are some things that moving water can do. Tell which term is associated with each great feat of water.

1. Rivers move at different speeds.

2. Water is drained from areas that share a system of channels.

3. Moving rivers roll heavy materials along the river bottom.

4. Moving rivers pick up lighter sediment and carry it along.

5. When the river profile flattens or the river meets an obstacle, it begins to wander from side to side across the flood plain.

6. As a moving river drags material along, it cuts a path into the rock.

7. A river deposits fertile soil on either side of its banks during floods.

8. Precipitation flows across Earth's surface and back into the ocean.

9. Water runs off rapidly from rocks that have no spaces for water to soak in.

10. Precipitation soaks into the ground and into rocks that have spaces between grains.

11. Moving water moves soil, particles, rocks, and debris— then drops it along the way.

12. Runoff carries loose material to the foot of a slope and drops the heaviest sediment first, then carries lighter sediment farther, dropping sediment in a triangular shape.

13. Water from high elevations flows in a network of rills, creeks, and streams into a river.

14. Rivers deposit sediment in their mouths in a fan shape as they empty into other bodies of water.

SEDIMENT
DRAINAGE BASIN
MEANDERING
IMPERMEABLE
BED LOAD
RUNOFF
FLOOD PLAIN
SUSPENDED LOAD
DELTA
CHANNEL
PERMEABLE
VELOCITY
ALLUVIAL FANS
DRAINAGE SYSTEM

Name

MOSTLY WATER

The surface of Earth is mostly water. Oceans, lakes, rivers, streams, ponds, icebergs, and glaciers cover ¾ of Earth's surface. Wiley Will Waters claims he's an expert on world water features. He's describing his visits to some of these places. Does he really know what he's talking about? For each of his descriptions, write YES or NO. If he's got his terms and features mixed up and an answer is NO, circle his misstatement and correct it on the line underneath.

_____ 1. "Today, I'm on the shores of the world's largest lake, Lake Superior."

_____

_____ 2. "Here we are at the source of the Amazon River, the place where it empties into the Atlantic Ocean."

_____

_____ 3. "This network of rills and creeks and streams which flow into the river is called a floodplain."

_____

_____ 4. "Here the river has overflowed its banks and deposited silt in the river channel."

_____

_____ 5. "The deposit dropped by this river in its mouth is called an aquifer."

_____

_____ 6. "This river, the Nile, is the world's longest river."

_____

_____ 7. "Sometimes a river wanders out of its bed and becomes a meandering river."

_____

_____ 8. "Some of Earth's water is under the surface, called groundwater."

_____

_____ 9. "The source of this river is the place where it began."

_____

_____ 10. "The Niagara River takes a steep plunge over this drop called a delta."

_____

_____ 11. "Rivers flow into their tributaries all over the world."

_____

_____ 12. "This oxbow lake was formed when a curve of a meandering river got cut off."

_____

_____ 13. "Here's the Pacific—the world's largest ocean."

_____

_____ 14. "This drainage system is the place where the river empties into a larger body of water."

_____

_____ 15. "This river has not flooded for a long time; it has stayed in its channel."

_____

Name _____

WHAT'S TRUE ABOUT GROUNDWATER?

Earth is actually a lot like a giant sponge. Water not only flows and moves around on the surface in rivers and lakes and oceans, it also collects and moves beneath the surface. The water that sinks into Earth's crust is called groundwater. Jocelyn has just taken a TRUE-FALSE test about groundwater. Grade her test. Give her 5 points for each correct answer. What is her final score?

___F___ 1. Groundwater flows faster than surface water.

___F___ 2. Water seeps into the ground until it reaches a rock layer with no pores.

___T___ 3. Gravity causes groundwater to move through connecting pores of Earth's crust.

___T___ 4. Some groundwater returns to the surface in springs.

___F___ 5. Often groundwater must be pumped to the surface to be used.

___F___ 6. Hot springs forced through small openings in Earth's crust are geysers.

___F___ 7. Groundwater is water that runs along Earth's surface.

___T___ 8. Stalactites are deposits hanging from cave roofs caused by dripping groundwater.

___F___ 9. Groundwater stops moving downward when it meets permeable rock.

___T___ 10. Some groundwater returns to the surface in swamps.

___T___ 11. Groundwater sometimes flows out of the surface in artesian wells.

___F___ 12. A funnel-shaped depression of limestone dissolved by rain is called a cave.

___F___ 13. Groundwater moves through permeable rock.

___T___ 14. Rainwater is weak acid that dissolves limestones and rock and creates caves.

___F___ 15. Calcium carbonate deposits on cave floors build up stalactites.

___T___ 16. Aquifers are permeable rock layers that are filled with water.

___F___ 17. Gravel and sand are good aquifers.

___F___ 18. Sinkholes are formed by meteors striking Earth's surface.

___F___ 19. The water table is just below the layer of impermeable rock.

___T___ 20. The water table is part of the zone of saturation.

Jocelyn's Score _____

Name _____

AWESOME ICE

Six million square miles of Earth's surface is covered by glaciers! That's 10% of Earth. Glaciers are huge masses of ice that move slowly on land. A glacier can carry massive amounts of rocks and other debris as it moves.

This glacier is filled with mixed-up glacial trivia. Match up the pairs that belong together. On the back of this page write the numbers 1–46. Beside each number, write the number of the trivia that matches it. (Each pair will be listed twice)

1
movement of glacial ice

2
melting water at base of glacier helps the ice move over land

3
layered deposits of glacial debris

4
large, deep crack in glacier surface

5
high, deep valleys formed by glaciers

6
glacial flow

7
ridges of debris left by melting water

8
horn

9
erosion

10
pressure causing ice layers to slide over each other

11
massive glaciers in polar regions that cover nearly all of Greenland and Antarctica

12
melt water

13
iceberg

14
basal flow

15
kettle lake

16
cirque

17
striations

18
crevasse

19
plucking

20
peak sharpened by glaciers

21
valley glacier

22
till

23
ice shelf

24
ground moraine

25
outwash

26
terminal moraine

27
plastic flow

28
abrading

29
debris dropped from base of glacier as it melts

30
small basins formed when blocks of ice surrounded by debris melt

31
scouring of bedrock surface by glacier

32
glaciers that extend onto a plain at the foot of a mountain

33
long, parallel scratches made by rocks dragged along by glaciers

34
mass of ice broken off a glacier

35
piedmont glacier

36
thick floating ice sheet attached to a continent

37
continental glaciers

38
moraines

39
hanging valleys

40
a process by which glacial water freezes around rocks as it moves

41
first material dropped by glacier—boulders, sand, clay

42
a hollow in which snow accumulates to form a valley glacier

43
alpine glacier formed in valleys at high elevations

44
water resulting from melting glaciers

45
ridges deposited at edges of glacier

46
how glaciers change Earth's surface

Name

DIGGING IN

No one has ever been able to dig into all the layers of Earth. If you could do it, you'd find things very different from what you see on the surface. Scientists have never gotten below the crust—so they can only use instruments to guess about what's inside. But they have some good ideas about Earth's layers. Pretend you are in the process of digging all the way to the center of Earth by answering these questions as you go! You'll need a science text or encyclopedia to help you answer some of the questions. Others can be answered from studying the diagram below.

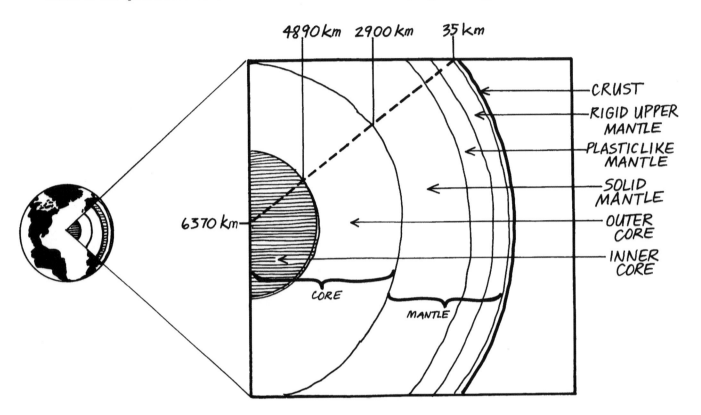

1. You're digging through the outermost layer. Where are you?_____

2. You reach the point where the mantle begins. What is it called? _____

3. You've gotten to about 100 km below the surface. Where are you?_____

4. The inside of Earth is very plasticlike here. Could you be in the mantle?_____

5. You're in a rocky, rigid layer. Where are you?_____

6. You're at the Gutenberg Discontinuity. Where are you? _____

7. You're close to the center, in a solid area. Where are you? _____

8. You're close to the center, but in a liquid area. Where are you? _____

9. You're in the crust, but only 5 km below the surface. What are you under?_____

10. You're in a near-fluid area about 200 km down. Where are you?_____

Name _____

THE AMAZING CRUST

A crust doesn't sound very exciting, does it? But the crust of Earth is a pretty amazing place. It is loaded with spectacular stuff. Get an atlas, an almanac, or an encyclopedia, and get to work finding out about some of the wonders of Earth's crust.

FIND EACH OF THESE:

1. the largest sand dunes
   Where? _____
   Height? _____

2. the biggest continent _____
   Area? _____

3. the largest volcanic crater
   Where? _____
   Area? _____

4. the highest mountain_____
   Height? _____

5. the highest active volcano
   Where? _____
   Height? _____

6. the longest glacier _____
   Where? _____

7. the deepest mine
   Where? _____
   Depth? _____

8. the biggest island _____
   Area? _____

9. the oldest rock
   Age? _____

10. the largest coral reef_____
    Length? _____

11. the largest lake _____
    Area? _____

12. the highest waterfall? _____
    Height? _____

13. highest sea wave
    Height? _____

14. largest cave system_____
    Length? _____

15. lowest point of land _____
    Depth below sea level? _____

16. deepest ocean trench _____
    Depth? _____

17. largest ocean_____
    Area? _____

18. largest tsunami
    Height? _____

TAKEN FOR "GRANITE"

Spewing, erupting volcanoes . . . high temperatures . . . tons of pressure . . . deposits of buried and hardened fragments . . . all of these lead to something we take for granted—the common (or not so common) ROCK! You might think rocks are pretty ordinary, not worth a lot of attention. Or you may be a serious rock hound (someone who loves, collects, and studies rocks). Whichever you are, it's good to know about rocks, because they're a pretty fundamental part of your world.

Show that you don't take rocks for granted by answering the questions on these two pages (42 and 43). You'll find some help on the rocks at the bottom of both pages. An answer may be used more than once.

1. What are the three big groups of rocks? _____

_____

2. Which rocks are formed from hardened lava that flowed from volcanoes? _____

3. What is the name of a very porous igneous rock that is so light that it floats? _____

4. What are the hollow ball-like objects, such as quartz, which are found in sedimentary rocks? _____

5. Which kind of metamorphic rocks are massive and lack banding?

_____

6. What happens to rock fragments that get buried after a long time?

_____

7. Which rocks have a name that means "fire"?

_____

8. What are the remains of once-living organisms found in sedimentary rocks?

_____

9. What are wavy features found on some sandstones? _____

10. What rocks are changed by high temperatures and high pressure?

_____

11. Name 4 kinds of sedimentary rocks._____

_____

12. What term is used to describe metamorphic rocks with a banded texture?

_____

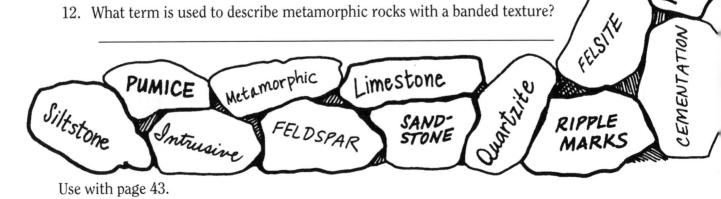

Use with page 43.

Name _____

Use with page 42.

13. What kinds of rocks are similar to layers of cake? _____

14. Basaltic magma would form what color of igneous rock? _____

15. What 2 groups of rocks are formed from all 3 kinds of rocks? _____

_____

16. What class of sedimentary rocks is made of fragments of rocks, minerals, and shells?

_____

17. Which igneous rocks are coarse-grained due to slow cooling? _____

18. Name 4 kinds of metamorphic rocks. _____

_____

19. What kinds of rocks are caused by weathering? _____

20. Name 4 kinds of igneous rocks. _____

_____

21. What is the class that includes sedimentary rocks which are deposited from a solution made by organic processes? _____

22. What metamorphic rock is commonly known as "coal"? _____

23. Which igneous rocks are fine-grained due to fast cooling? _____

24. What process happens when mud or silt is buried and water and air are squeezed out, producing such rocks as shale? _____

25. What process happens when minerals are precipitated out of water and hold particles of rock together? _____

26. What rocks are a mix of rounded pebbles and sand? _____

27. What rocks are a mix of sharp, angular pebbles? _____

28. What sedimentary rock is formed from thin layers of clay compacted very tightly together? _____

29. Where is the precipitate calcite commonly found to create interesting formations in the ground? _____

30. What animals secrete calcite around their bodies, forming massive reefs?

_____

harden
GEODES
BRECCIA
CONGLOMERATE
Granite
CORALS
IGNEOUS
SHALE
CAVES
SEDIMENTARY
nonfoliated
FOLIATED
COMPACTION
LIGHT
CLASTIC
basalt
NON-CLASTIC
SLATE

Name _____

TREASURES IN THE EARTH

Earth's crust is loaded with minerals—some of them common, some of them very rare. Even those that don't cost hundreds or thousands of dollars in the gem variety are valuable and useful. All minerals are natural, inorganic solids which have interesting crystalline structures. Each mineral is a specific combination of elements. Minerals are usually identified by certain physical properties such as hardness, streak, luster, mass, form, cleavage, feel, smell, and taste.

Erik and Erika, two young mineral fanatics, have discovered some treasures. Answer the questions on these two pages (44 and 45) about what they have found. To do this you will need to pay attention to the hardness scale below. You will also need the chart of "Physical Properties of Some Common Minerals" from page 56.

1. Erika has found a mineral that scratches quartz. Could it be gypsum? _____

2. The searchers are thrilled to find a handful of pale yellow, shiny nuggets. They are sure they have found gold! The mineral leaves a green-ish-black streak, and cannot be scratched by fluorite. Have they struck it rich? _____

3. Erik has a handful of whitish-gray stones with a nonmetallic luster that leave a colorless streak. They can be scratched by a steel file but not by a knife. What does he have? _____

4. Both kids have found samples of a red mineral which leaves a gray streak. It can be scratched with a fingernail and with a penny, and it can be easily cut with a knife. What is it? _____

5. Erika is holding a very soft mineral that leaves black "grease" on her fingers. It makes a black streak and has a shiny luster. What is it? _____

6. Erik has found a metallic, gray mineral that leaves a gray streak. The crystals appear cubic. When it breaks, it breaks with clear, clean cleavage. It scratches gypsum. Is it graphite?_____

7. Erika has a pile of white, nonmetallic stones that leave a white streak. They can be scratched with a fingernail. What are they? _____

8. Erik has some yellow stones that leave a yellow streak. They can be scratched with a fingernail. He wonders if they could be gold, but they do not have a metallic luster. What might they be?

9. A pale white stone is found at Erik's feet. It has hexagonal crystals, leaves a white streak, and can be scratched by a knife, but not by a finger-nail. Could it be dolomite? _____

HARDNESS SCALE

Hardness	Characteristics and Example
1	soft, greasy, flakes on fingers (talc)
2	can be scratched by fingernail (gypsum)
3	can be cut easily with a knife or nail, or scratched by a penny (calcite)
4	can be scratched easily by a knife (fluorite)
5	can be scratched by a knife with difficulty (apatite)
6	can be scratched by a steel file (orthoclase)
7	scratches a steel file (quartz)
8	scratches quartz (topaz)
9	scratches anything lower on scale (corundum)
10	scratches anything lower on scale (diamond)

Use with page 45.

Name _____

Use with page 44.

10. Erik has picked up a mineral which feels soapy and leaves a white, powdery residue on his hands. It is very soft and flakes off. What has he probably found? _____

11. Meanwhile, Erika has a colorless chunk that breaks apart into cubes. It has no luster and is soft enough to be scratched by fluorite. When she gets it wet, it starts to dissolve. What has she found? _____

12. Right away, Erika finds another colorless chunk of mineral. It cannot be scratched by calcite. It has no shine to it, and seems to break apart in many directions. What has she probably found? _____

13. The two have stumbled upon a large amount of a mineral that has various colors. Some of it is almost clear. It appears to have hexagonal crystals and is hard enough to scratch a steel file. What could it be? _____

14. Erik has found a deep red mineral that looks like a gem. It leaves a colorless streak and is harder than quartz. Could it be a garnet? ____

15. A brown mineral that leaves a brown streak is in Erika's basket. It fractures irregularly, and can be scratched by a steel file but not by a knife. It has a nonmetallic luster. What might it be? _____

16. Erika is especially excited about a find of whitish mineral that glows when she puts it under ultraviolet light. It leaves a colorless streak and cannot be scratched with a penny, but can be scratched with a knife. What might it be? _____

17. Erik's mother has let him examine a gem she has. It is blue, leaves a colorless streak, and cannot be scratched with anything they find. It does scratch quartz. What might it be?

_____

DRUSY QUARTZ

CITRINE QUARTZ

SMOKY QUARTZ

ROSE QUARTZ

AMETHYST QUARTZ

18. Erica thinks she's found some copper. The mineral looks coppery-red, and can be scratched by fluorite. It has a metallic luster. Is this probably copper? _____

19. Another black mineral is in Erik's basket. It leaves a black streak and has a metallic luster. It cannot be scratched by a fingernail, knife, or penny. Is it galena? _____

20. A yellow gem that Erika has seems to be a topaz. If it is, will it scratch a steel file? _____

21. The pair has happened upon a small amount of a shiny, silvery-white mineral that leaves a light gray streak. It is hard enough to scratch calcite. Could it be silver? _____

22. Erika has a green, nonmetallic mineral that leaves a colorless streak. It can be scratched by a penny, but not easily by a fingernail. Could it be muscovite? _____

Name _____

WHICH VOLCANO?

One volcano is not necessarily like every other volcano. Did you know that there are different sorts of volcanoes? There are—because not all volcanoes look or behave alike or throw out the same stuff at the same speed. Read up on volcanoes so you can decide which description and which picture belongs with which kind of volcano. (A volcano is a crack or vent in Earth's crust through which lava or magma is expelled.)

LABELS:

STRATOVOLCANO
Description #: _____ Picture #: _____

SHIELD VOLCANO
Description #: _____ Picture #: _____

CINDER CONE VOLCANO
Description #: _____ Picture #: _____

DOME VOLCANO
Description #: _____ Picture #: _____

1. The most common form of volcano, this kind is made of layers of lava and ash, cinders and rock fragments. A quiet lava flow seals off solid lava inside. The pressure builds up and results in violent eruptions. Mt. Fuji in Japan and Mt. Vesuvius in Italy are examples of this kind of volcano.

2. This kind of volcano has a low, broad look. It is formed by basalt flowing quietly out of a central opening. The lava flows out over gently sloping sides. These volcanoes can grow to be very large and spread out over a huge area. The Hawaiian Islands are built of this kind of volcano.

3. These are cone-shaped hills that are very steep. This kind of volcano is formed by violent eruptions that blow out fragments of lava in fine cinders. The cinders build up around the vent to make a very steep cone. Mt. Pelee in Martinique and Mt. Capulin in New Mexico are examples of this kind of volcano.

4. This volcano has slower-flowing lava. Although the sides are very steep, the volcanoes are smaller. This kind of volcano has a dome-shaped mass in the crater.

Name

FOLDS & FAULTS & QUAKES

Are you puzzled by the folds and cracks and quivers and shakes of Earth's surface? Well, you don't have to be for long. Get out your science book or an encyclopedia and brush up on the features and terms related to faults, folds, and earthquakes. Then take a hard look at this puzzle. You'll notice that the puzzle is already done for you! Oh, but something is missing—the clues to the puzzle. It's your job to create them. Use the spaces provided at the bottom.

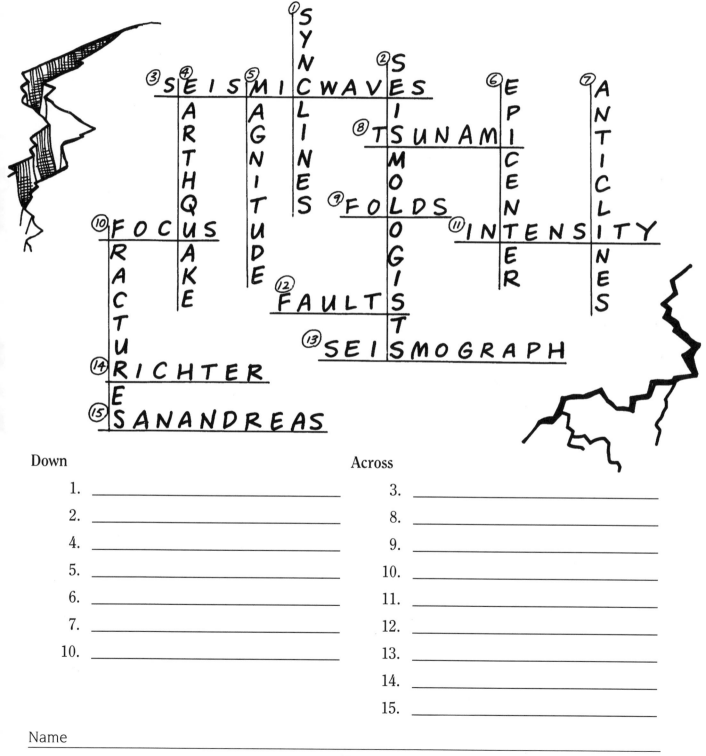

Down

1. _____
2. _____
4. _____
5. _____
6. _____
7. _____
10. _____

Across

3. _____
8. _____
9. _____
10. _____
11. _____
12. _____
13. _____
14. _____
15. _____

Name _____

GIANT PLATES

Earth's crust is made up of many huge pieces like a gigantic jigsaw puzzle. Each piece is a giant plate. Continents and oceans rest on these plates, which are always on the move. They are constantly being pulled apart or pushed together, or they are colliding with each other. Fit together the puzzle pieces that belong. There are eleven pairs of matching terms and descriptions in the puzzle pieces below. For each number (1–22), list the matching puzzle piece. (Each pair will be listed twice.)

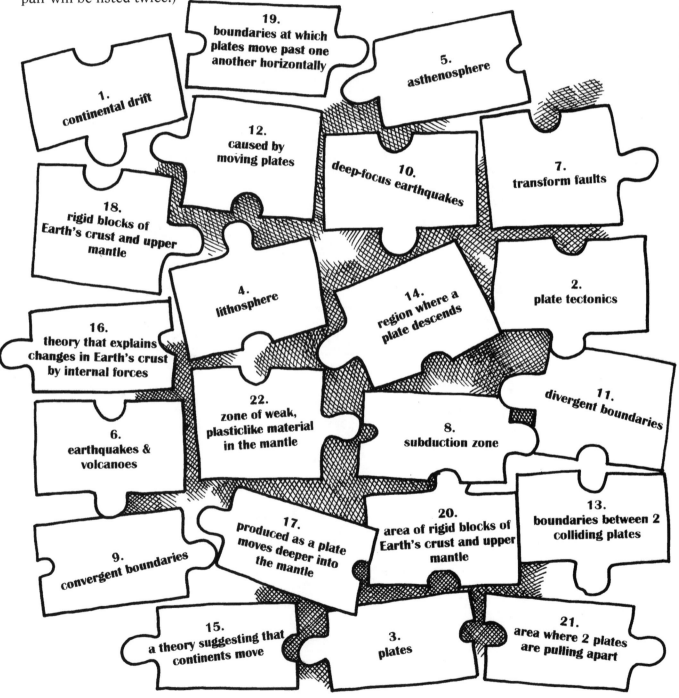

19. boundaries at which plates move past one another horizontally

5. asthenosphere

1. continental drift

12. caused by moving plates

10. deep-focus earthquakes

7. transform faults

18. rigid blocks of Earth's crust and upper mantle

4. lithosphere

14. region where a plate descends

2. plate tectonics

16. theory that explains changes in Earth's crust by internal forces

22. zone of weak, plasticlike material in the mantle

8. subduction zone

11. divergent boundaries

6. earthquakes & volcanoes

17. produced as a plate moves deeper into the mantle

20. area of rigid blocks of Earth's crust and upper mantle

13. boundaries between 2 colliding plates

9. convergent boundaries

15. a theory suggesting that continents move

3. plates

21. area where 2 plates are pulling apart

Name _____

48

GREAT QUAKES & ERUPTIONS

Can you find out about some of Earth's most devastating earthquakes, most damaging volcanoes, longest earthquakes, most active volcanoes? Get a good almanac or encyclopedia, and see what you can learn about these earthquakes and volcanoes.

EARTHQUAKES

Write what you can find out about the magnitude, length, and damage of each "quake."

1923　Tokyo _____

1927　China _____

1939　Chile _____

1970　Peru _____

1976　China _____

1980　Italy _____

1989　San Francisco _____

1992　Turkey _____

1993　India _____

1994　California _____

1995　Japan _____

VOLCANOES

Write what you can find out about these eruptions and their damage.

A.D. 79　Mt. Vesuvius, Italy _____

1669　Mt. Etna, Sicily _____

1792　Mt. Unzen, Japan _____

1815　Mt. Tambora, Indonesia _____

1883　Mt. Krakotoa, Indonesia _____

1902　Mt. Pelée, Martinique _____

1906　Mt. Vesuvius, Italy _____

1980　Mt. St. Helens, Oregon, USA _____

1984　Mt. Mauna Loa, Hawaii _____

1985　Nevado del Ruiz, Colombia _____

SUCH ODD STUFF!

There are some strange, mysterious features on and just below Earth's surface. Find out what these mysteries are. (See the list below.) Which mysterious sight would you be near in each of these examples?

A. HOT SPRINGS

B. FUMORALE

C. GEYSER

D. LACCOLITH

E. VOLCANIC NECK

F. SINKHOLE

G. CALDERA

H. MUDSPOTS

I. SOLFATARAS

J. BATHOLITH

K. DIKE

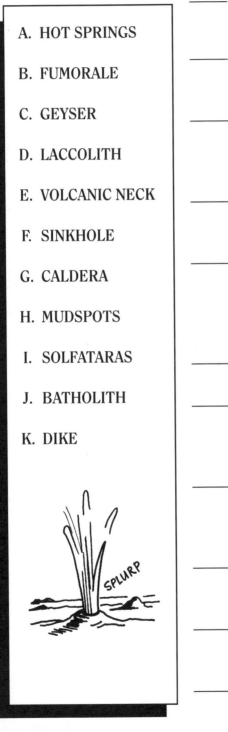

_____ 1. You take a swim in a lake-filled crater formed when a volcano blew its top and the volcano's cone collapsed into the vent.

_____ 2. You are filming a natural hot spring that is shooting hot water high up into the air through a small opening in Earth's surface.

_____ 3. Your cousin is videotaping you as you relax in a steaming hot pool of underground water which was heated by magma in a thermal region before it rose through cracks into the pool.

_____ 4. You're recording the strange popping noises as you watch the plopping, spurting patterns made by hot water squirting up through mud.

_____ 5. You hold your nose because this spot smells like rotten eggs. It's an outlet in Earth's surface where steam, chlorides, sulfurs, and other gases are given off by cooling magma. The rocks around the edges are yellow from the sulfur, and wow! Does it smell!

_____ 6. More rotten eggs! This dying volcano gives off sulfur vapors all the time.

_____ 7. You have to envision this one, because it's beneath the surface. A large mass of intrusive igneous rock forms the core of a mountain you're admiring. This solid mass extends far down into Earth.

_____ 8. You saw it with your own eyes! A road disappeared, and a truck with it—into a funnel-shaped depression in the earth caused by dissolving limestone beneath the surface.

_____ 9. Another underground marvel—a mushroom-shaped body of igneous rock, formed as lava hardens in this strange shape.

_____ 10. The earth has eroded away to leave a tall skinny mass of rock that was formed underground when magma entered a vertical crack and hardened.

_____ 11. An inactive volcano had magma solidified in its pipe. As the softer, outer rock wore away, this remained resistant to erosion.

Name

APPENDIX

CONTENTS

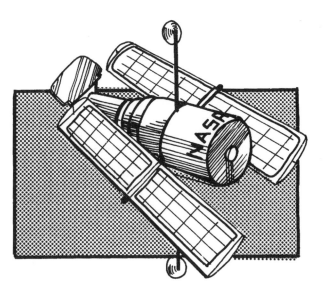

EARTH & SPACE SCIENCE GLOSSARY

abrading: scouring of the bedrock by a glacier

abrasion: a scouring action of wind-carried particles resulting in the erosion of rock surfaces

absolute magnitude: a measure of a star's actual brightness

abyss: ocean depths of 2000 to 6000 meters

abyssal plain: the flat, almost level area of the ocean basin

acid precipitation: rain or snow that forms as the result of mixture of air pollutants with moisture in the atmosphere

air mass: a body of air that has the same properties as the region over which it develops

aneroid barometer: an instrument used to measure air pressure

anthracite: the final stage in coal formation

anticyclone: an air mass in which air circulates away from the center in a clockwise motion in the Northern Hemisphere

aphelion: the point in an orbit when an object is farthest from the sun

apparent magnitude: the brightness of a star observed at its actual distance from Earth

apparent motion: the motion of an object relative to the position of its observer

aquifers: permeable rocks containing water

artesian well: a well in which water is under pressure due to the weight of the overlying column of water in the aquifer

asteroids: fragments of matter similar to planetary matter that orbit between Mars and Jupiter

asthenosphere: the upper, plasticlike portion of the mantle

astronomical unit (AU): the average distance between Earth and the sun; used to measure distances within the solar system

astronomy: the study of objects in space

atoll: a coral reef that surrounds a lagoon

authigenic deposits: deposits that form in place

barometer: an instrument used to measure air pressure

barrier islands: sand deposits that parallel the shore but are separated from the mainland

barrier reef: a coral reef that is separated from a landmass by water

basalt: a dark-colored extrusive igneous rock

basaltic magma: magma that originates in the mantle and flows readily

batholiths: large masses of intrusive igneous rock extending to unknown depths; often form cores of mountains

bed load: sediment that is rolled along a river bottom

bedrock: the solid rock found under soil

Big Bang: a theory stating that the universe originated from the explosion of a huge mass of matter

binary star: two stars revolving around a common center

black hole: a star in which matter is condensed and its gravity field so strong that light cannot escape

body waves: waves traveling outward from the focus of an earthquake in all directions through Earth's interior

Ceres: the largest asteroid, discovered in 1801

cinder cones: steep-sided volcanoes formed by violent eruptions

cirque: the original hollow in which snow accumulates to form a valley glacier

cirrus: a high, white, feathery cloud composed of ice crystals or supercooled water; associated with fair weather

clastics: sedimentary rocks made of rock fragments, minerals, and broken shells

clay: a fine sediment formed from chemical weathering of either iron-magnesium minerals or feldspars

cleavage: a physical property that describes the way a mineral breaks

climate: the average of all weather conditions of an area over a long period of time

cold front: the boundary developed when a cold air mass meets a warm air mass

coma: a cloud of dust and gas that forms a halo around the nucleus of a comet

comet: a mass of frozen gases, cosmic dust, and small rock particles that orbits the sun

compaction: a process by which sediments become consolidated into rocks

compression: a system of forces that pushes against a body from directly opposite sides

consolidation: process in which materials are compressed into a compact mass

constellations: groups or patterns of stars

contact metamorphism: changes in rocks that occur as the result of an intruding magma body

continental drift: a hypothesis that suggests the continents have been in different positions through geologic time

continental glacier: a large ice sheet whose movement is outward due to pressure from overlying ice and snow

continental shelf: the relatively flat part of a continent that is covered by seawater

continental slope: the steeply dipping surface between the outer edge of the continental shelf and the ocean basin

convergent boundaries: boundaries between two colliding plates

core: the inner part of the sun where fusion occurs; also the innermost part of Earth

corona: the transparent zone beyond the chromosphere of the sun visible only during a total solar eclipse

craters: depressions on the surfaces of some planets and their moons

crest: the highest point of a wave

crust: the outermost layer of Earth that extends from the surface to a depth of about 35 kilometers

crystal: a solid bounded by plane surfaces that has a definite shape due to its internal arrangement

cumulus: a thick, puffy cloud that develops when rising columns of moist air are cooled to the dew point

cyclones: low-pressure systems in Northern Hemisphere; air circulates toward the center in a counterclockwise motion

decomposition: the chemical process of weathering

deep-focus earthquake: earthquake that occurs in the mantle in the rigid, descending plate

deep-sea trenches: parts of the ocean floor where an oceanic plate has been subducted and descends into the mantle

deep-water wave: a wave moving in water that is deeper than one-half of its wavelength

delta: a fan-shaped deposit that accumulates when a moving body of water loses its velocity

density current: a current formed by the movement of more dense water toward an area of less dense water

deposition: the process by which products of erosion are laid down

desert: a hot, dry area of land receiving less than 25 centimeters of rainfall annually

dew point: the temperature at which condensation occurs

dikes: rock structures formed when magma enters a vertical fracture in rock and hardens

disintegration: the physical or mechanical process of weathering

diurnal: an event occurring once a day; usually refers to the tides

Basic Skills/Earth & Space Science 6-8+

divergent boundaries: boundaries where two plates are pulling apart

doldrums: a windless zone at the equator

dome volcanoes: small, steep-sided volcanoes made from rhyolitic lava

drainage basin: an area separated by divides and drained by the major water body of the region

drainage system: a network of channels that joins to form the main water body

drought: a long period of little or no precipitation

earthquakes: vibrations caused by the sudden movement of surface rocks

Earth science: the study of planet Earth and its place in space

eclipse: the passing of one object into the shadow of another

epicenter: the point at Earth's surface that is directly above the focus of an earthquake

equator: an imaginary line that lies halfway between the North and South Poles

equinox: either of the two times each year when the sun crosses the equator, and day and night are of equal length

eras: the largest subdivisions of geologic time

erosion: the process by which Earth materials are carried away and are deposited by wind, water, gravity, or ice

evaporation: process by which a liquid becomes a gas

extinction: the total disappearance of a species

extrusive igneous rocks: rocks formed when lava cools at or near Earth's surface

faults: fractures in a rock body along which movement has taken place

first quarter: a phase of the moon when sun, Earth, and moon form a right angle; moon appears half bright and half dark

floodplain: an area of fertile soil composed of fine sediment deposited during floods

focus: the actual point on a fault where movement occurs and vibrations begin

fog: a stratus cloud close to Earth's surface formed from the condensation of water vapor

folded mountains: mountains that form as the result of compression

folds: bends in a rock layer due to force

fossils: the remains or traces of once-living organisms preserved in Earth's rocks

fracture: a distinct manner of breaking in a mineral other than along planar surfaces; a break in a rock body due to force

freezing point: the temperature at which liquids change to solids

frequency: the number of waves that pass a given point per second

full moon: phase of the moon that occurs when Earth is between the sun and the moon, side of the moon facing Earth is bright

galaxies: large systems of stars, gases, and dust

gems: rare minerals that are highly prized due to their color, luster, and hardness

geodes: hollow, ball-like objects found in some sedimentary rocks

geologic map: a map showing the outcrop areas of rock units, structural features, and ages of surface rocks

geologic time scale: a chronological arrangement or sequence of events of Earth's history

geologists: scientists who study the processes that form and change Earth

geology: the study of all processes affecting Earth

geothermal energy: energy that comes from the internal heat of Earth

geysers: hot springs that erupt water and steam at regular intervals

glaciers: thick masses of ice in motion

gravity: the attraction between two objects due to their masses; an agent of erosion

Great Red Spot: the gaseous, hurricane-like mass on the planet Jupiter

ground moraine: debris deposited from the base of an ice sheet as it melts

groundwater: water that sinks into the porous areas of the crust

halite: table salt

hanging valleys: U-shaped scars that form when a glacial tributary enters the main valley above its base

hardness: a mineral's resistance to being scratched

humus: material formed from decayed organic matter; found in topsoil

hurricanes: storms that develop when warm, moist air carried by trade winds rotates around a low-pressure "eye"

hydrosphere: the waters of Earth including oceans, lakes, rivers, groundwater, snow, ice and glaciers, and water vapor

ice age: a period of time when ice sheets and alpine glaciers were far more extensive than they are today

igneous rock: rock formed from molten Earth material

impermeable: a condition of a rock or soil in which fluids cannot move through the tightly packed particles

inner planets: the planets relatively close to the sun—Mercury, Venus, Earth, and Mars

intensity: a measure of the surface damage caused by an earthquake

interglacial period: a length of time characterized by warm or mild climates that separates periods of widespread glaciation

intrusive igneous rocks: rocks formed when magma cools slowly beneath Earth's surface

ionosphere: the lower zone of the thermosphere that contains ions and free electrons

jet streams: narrow belts of wind near the tropopause that form when warm tropical air meets cold polar air

lagoon: a shallow sound near a larger body of water

land breeze: a circulation pattern in which warm air over water rises and is replaced by cooler air from land; occurs at night

landslides: rapid downhill movements of large amounts of Earth materials

last quarter: a phase of the moon in which the moon is waning

latitude: a parallel line that identifies locations or distances north or south of the equator

lava: magma that is released at Earth's surface during volcanic eruptions

leaching: the process by which some soil components are dissolved and carried downward by water

leeward: away from the wind

levee: a low ridge of coarse sediment deposited by a river along its margins

light-year: a measure of the distance light travels in one year, equal to 9.5×10^{12} km

lithosphere: rigid blocks of crustal and mantle material of which the continents are a part

loess: a windblown deposit of fine dust particles gathered from deserts, dry riverbeds, or old glacial lakebeds

longitude: a line perpendicular to the equator used to identify distances or locations east or west of the prime meridian

lunar eclipse: an eclipse that occurs when the moon passes into Earth's shadow

luster: a physical property that refers to the way light is reflected from a mineral's surface

magma: molten material found beneath Earth's surface

magnetic pole: either of two regions located in the polar areas and toward which a compass needle points

magnitude: a measure of the strength of an earthquake

mantle: the middle layer of Earth located between the crust and the core

meltwater: water resulting from the melting of glacial snow and ice

meridians: lines of longitude that pass through the poles

mesas: flat-topped hills covered by a resistant rock layer protecting soft rock underneath

mesosphere: the coldest zone of the atmosphere; extends upward from Earth from approximately 50–80 kilometers

metallic: having a shiny luster; resembling a metal

metals: materials valuable because of their malleability and conductivity

metamorphic rocks: rocks that form from pre-existing rocks as the result of temperature and pressure changes

meteorites: small fragments of matter that strike Earth

meteoroids: small fragments of matter moving through space that vaporize upon entering Earth's atmosphere

meteorologist: a scientist who studies storm patterns and climates in order to predict daily weather

meteorology: the study of weather and the forces and processes that cause it

meteors: meteoroids that burn up in Earth's atmosphere

mid-ocean ridge: an underwater mountain chain that rises from the ocean basins

Milky Way: the spiral galaxy to which Earth and the rest of our solar system belong

mineral: a naturally occurring, inorganic, crystalline solid, with a definite chemical composition

mudflows: rapid, downhill movements of materials occurring after heavy rains

neap tides: low tides that occur when the sun, Earth, and moon form a right angle

nebula: a low-density cloud of gas and dust in which a star is born

new moon: a phase of the moon in which the side of the moon facing Earth is dark

nimbus: a dark gray cloud with ragged edges from which rain or snow continually falls

nonmetallic: having a dull, pearly, silky, glassy, or brilliant luster

nonrenewable resources: materials from Earth's crust that cannot be recycled or replaced within a useful period of time

nova: an ordinary star that suddenly increases in brightness and then fades slowly back to its original brightness

oasis: a fertile, green area in an arid region

occluded front: a boundary that forms when two cold air masses merge, forcing the warmer air between them to rise

oceanic trench: a deep trough on the ocean basin floor

oceanographers: scientists who study the properties of ocean water and the processes that occur within oceans

oceanography: the study of Earth's oceans

orbit: the path followed by a planet

ores: minerals or rock deposits that can be mined for a profit

orogeny: the processes involved in mountain building

outer planets: the giant, gaseous planets—Jupiter, Saturn, Uranus, Neptune, and Pluto

outwash: sorted, layered deposits of glacial debris

penumbra: a partial shadow formed during an eclipse

perihelion: the point in an orbit when an object is closest to the sun

periods: geologic time units that are subdivisions of eras

permeable: a condition of some rocks in which pore spaces exist within the rock thus allowing fluids to move through the rock

petrified: a form of fossil preservation in which organic material is replaced by minerals from ground water

photosphere: the visible surface of the sun

piedmont glacier: a glacier that forms at the foot of a mountain when valley glaciers advance onto the plain

plains: vast, flat areas of low elevation

planet: an object in space that reflects light from a nearby star around which it revolves

plateaus: high, relatively flat areas next to mountains

plates: rigid blocks of Earth's crust and upper mantle

plate tectonics: a theory that explains movements of continents and changes in Earth's crust caused by internal forces

polar easterlies: cold, dry, dense air located between the poles and 60° latitude

Polaris: North Star

polar zone: a cold climate zone that extends from the poles to 66½° north and south latitudes

precipitates: nonclastic sedimentary rocks that form when solids settle out of solution

precipitation: water that falls to Earth's surface from the atmosphere as rain, snow, hail, or sleet

prevailing westerlies: winds located between about 30° and 60° latitude in the Northern Hemisphere

prime meridian: the meridian that passes through Greenwich, England (0° longitude), from which distances east and west on Earth's surface are measured

real motion: the actual movement of an object

red giants: stars near the end of their existence whose cores collapse due to an exhaustion of hydrogen

reflecting telescope: an instrument in which light collects on a concave mirror; reflects magnified image in eyepiece

refracting telescopes: instruments that use an objective lens to bend light toward the focal plane where the image is formed

relative dating: a method that places an event in its proper order by comparing the event with other chronological events

relative motion: the motion of one object as compared to the motion of another object

retrograde motion: the apparent westward movement of a planet as seen from Earth

revolution: the circling of one object about another

Richter scale: an expression of earthquake magnitudes as measured by seismographs

rift zone: a system of cracks in Earth's crust through which molten material rises

rip currents: narrow currents that flow seaward at a right angle to the shoreline

rock cycle: the changes that rocks undergo from the magmatic state, to rocks, and back to magma

rockets: action-reaction engines based on Newton's third law of motion

rocks: Earth materials made of one or more minerals

rotation: the turning motion of an object on its axis

runoff: precipitation that flows across a land surface as drainage

sand dunes: hills of sand deposited by the wind when it slows down or meets an obstacle

satellite: an object that revolves around a large primary body

sea level: the level of the surface of the sea midway between the average high and low tides

seamount: a volcano that does not rise above sea level

sedimentary rocks: rocks formed as the result of weathering and redisposition of loose Earth materials

sediments: loose Earth materials or debris resulting from weathering

seismic waves: vibrations that result when rock suddenly breaks and moves, releasing large amounts of energy

seismographs: instruments that record Earth tremors

seismologists: scientists who study earthquakes

semidiurnal: having two high tides and two low tides each day

shallow-focus earthquakes: earthquakes produced at the outer edge of ocean trenches, as rocks are folded into mountains, at transform faults, and at mid-ocean ridges

shallow-water wave: a wave moving in water that is shallower than one-half its wavelength

shearing: a system of forces that pushes against a body from different sides not directly opposite each other

shore zone: the area lying between high and low tides

sill: a horizontal sheet of rock formed when magma intrudes two rock layers and hardens

silt: sediment smaller than sand

sinkholes: funnel-shaped depressions that result from the dissolution of limestone along cracks and joints

smog: a foglike pollution made darker and more dense by smoke and chemical fumes

soil: a mixture of weathered rock and decayed organic material

solar eclipse: an eclipse that occurs when Earth is in the moon's shadow

solar energy: energy from the sun

solar flares: sudden increases in brightness of the sun's chromosphere

solar system: a system of objects in orbit around our sun

solstice: either of two points where the sun reaches its maximum distances north and south of the equator

spacelab: a workshop and laboratory located in the cargo bay of a space shuttle

space probes: rocket-launched vehicles that carry data-gathering equipment above Earth's atmosphere

space shuttle: a reusable craft designed to transport astronaut, materials, and satellites to and from space

space station: a space that contains all the equipment & life-support systems necessary for astronauts to live & work in space

spectroscope: an instrument that separates visible light into its various wavelengths

spring tides: tides that occur when the sun, moon, and Earth align

stack: an island of resistant rock left after weaker rock is worn away by waves and currents

stalactites: elongated structures of calcium carbonate that hang from cave ceilings

stalagmites: upward growths of calcium carbonate from a cave floor

stars: hot, bright spheres of gas

stationary front: a boundary that forms when either a warm front or a cold front stops moving forward

stratosphere: a layer of the atmosphere that contains the ozone layer

stratus: a layered cloud, often covering the whole sky, associated with light drizzle

streak: the color of a powdered mineral

striation: a glacial scratch or groove left in bedrock as ice moves over it

sunspots: relatively cool, dark areas on the sun's surface

supergiants: red giant stars

supernova: a star whose sudden increase in brightness indicates a greater outburst of energy than a nova

surf: the result of the forming and breaking of many waves

surface currents: movements of water as a result of wind

surface waves: tremors that travel along Earth's surface

suspended load: sediment picked up and carried by a river

talus: material that collects at the foot of a steep slope or cliff

temperate zone: a climate zone between the tropics and the polar zones where weather changes with the season

temperature: a measure of the amount of heat in an object

terminal moraines: ridges of glacial till left at the margins of an ice sheet

thermal pollution: the result of returning heated water to its source

thermosphere: the outermost layer of the atmosphere that extends from about 80 kilometers upward into space

thrust: a force produced by the expansion of hot gases that propels a rocket forward

tidal power: the use of ocean tides to produce electricity

tidal range: the difference between high tide and low tide

tides: shallow water waves caused by the gravitational attraction among Earth, moon, and sun

till: an unsorted, unlayered glacial deposit of boulders, sand, and clay

topography: the surface features of an area

topsoil: the uppermost layer of soil

tornado: a violent, whirling wind that moves in a narrow path over land

trade winds: winds that blow toward the equator from about 30° north and south of the doldrums

transform faults: boundaries at which plates move past one another horizontally

tremors: seismic vibrations

tropics: a climate zone lying between 23° N and S latitude that receives the greatest concentration of sunlight

tropopause: the boundary near the top of the troposphere that acts as a ceiling to the weather zone

troposphere: a layer of the atmosphere nearest Earth, containing 75 percent of the gases of the atmosphere

trough: the lowest point of a wave

tsunamis: seismic sea waves

U-shaped valley: a valley eroded by a valley glacier

umbra: an inner complete shadow formed during an eclipse

upwelling: the rising of cold, deep ocean water toward the surface, especially along continental coasts

valley glaciers: glaciers that form at high elevations from year-round snow in hollows or valleys; also called alpine glaciers

variable stars: stars that change brightness

volcano: a mountain formed by the accumulation of material that has been forced out of Earth's interior onto its surface

warm front: a boundary that develops when a less dense, warm air mass meets a denser, colder air mass

warning: a weather advisory issued when severe weather conditions exist

watch: a weather advisory issued when conditions are such that severe weather could occur

water table: the upper surface of a zone of saturation

wave base: the depth of water equal to one-half the wavelength of a wave

wave height: the vertical distance between the crest and trough of a wave

wavelength: the horizontal distance between successive wave crests or troughs

wave period: the time it takes two successive wave crests to pass a given point

weathering: all processes by which rocks change at or near Earth's surface

white dwarf: the dying core of a giant that radiates heat into space as light waves

windward: facing into the wind

PHYSICAL PROPERTIES OF SOME COMMON MINERALS

Metallic Luster

MINERAL	COLOR	STREAK	HARDNESS	CRYSTALS	BREAKAGE
GRAPHITE	black to gray	black to gray	1–2	hexagonal	scales
SILVER	silvery, white	light gray to silver	2.5	cubic	hackly
GALENA	gray	gray to black	2.5	cubic	perfect, cubic
GOLD	pale-golden yellow	yellow	2.5–3	cubic	hackly
COPPER	copper red	copper red	3	cubic	hackly
CHROMITE	black or brown	brown to black	5.5	cubic	irregular
MAGNETITE	black	black	6	cubic	conchoidal
PYRITE	light brassy yellow	greenish black	6.5	cubic	uneven

Nonmetallic Luster

MINERAL	COLOR	STREAK	HARDNESS	CRYSTALS	BREAKAGE
TALC	white, greenish	white	1	monoclinic	in 1 direction
BAUXITE	gray, red, brown, white	gray	1–3	—	—
GYPSUM	colorless, gray, white	white	2	monoclinic	basal cleavage
SULFUR	yellow	yellow to white	2	orthorhombic	conchoidal
MUSCOVITE	white, gray, yellow, rose, green	colorless	2.5	monoclinic	basal cleavage
HALITE	colorless, red, white, blue	colorless	2.5	cubic	cubic
CALCITE	colorless, white	colorless, white	3	hexagonal	in 3 directions
DOLOMITE	colorless, white, pink, green, gray	white	3.5–4	hexagonal	in 3 directions
FLUORITE	colorless, white, blue, green, red, yellow, purple	colorless	4	cubic	cleavage
HORNBLENDE	green to black	gray to white	5–6	monoclinic	in 2 directions
FELDSPAR	gray, green, white	colorless	6	monoclinic	2 planes
QUARTZ	colorless, colors	colorless	7	hexagonal	conchoidal
GARNET	yellow-red, green, black	colorless	7.5	cubic	conchoidal
TOPAZ (gemstone)	white, pink, yellow, blue, colorless	colorless	8	orthorhombic	basal
CORUNDUM	colorless, blue, brown,	colorless	9	hexagonal	fracture

Basic Skills/Earth & Space Science 6-8+

EARTH & SPACE SCIENCE
SKILLS TEST

Each correct answer is worth 1 point.

Questions 1–20: Match each term with its definition.

_____ 1. loess
_____ 2. core
_____ 3. gibbous
_____ 4. geyser
_____ 5. salinity
_____ 6. front
_____ 7. impermeable
_____ 8. sediment
_____ 9. latitude
_____ 10. delta
_____ 11. trough
_____ 12. aquifers
_____ 13. erosion
_____ 14. diurnal
_____ 15. neap
_____ 16. umbra
_____ 17. corona
_____ 18. equinox
_____ 19. meteorites
_____ 20. fault

a boundary where two air masses meet
b distance north or south of the equator
c time of year when day and night are the same length
d meteors that strike the ground
e crack in Earth's crust
f innermost layer of Earth
g phase where more than ¼ of the moon is visible
h tides that occur when sun, moon, and Earth are at right angles
i Earth's materials are carried away
j hot springs that regularly erupt water & steam
k sediment deposit at mouth of river
l inner shadow in an eclipse
m windblown deposit of dust
n low point of a wave
o outer zone of the sun's surface
p occurs daily
q permeable rocks containing water
r water cannot soak in
s concentration of salt
t loose earth material resulting from weathering

21. What moon phase is shown in the diagram below?

_____

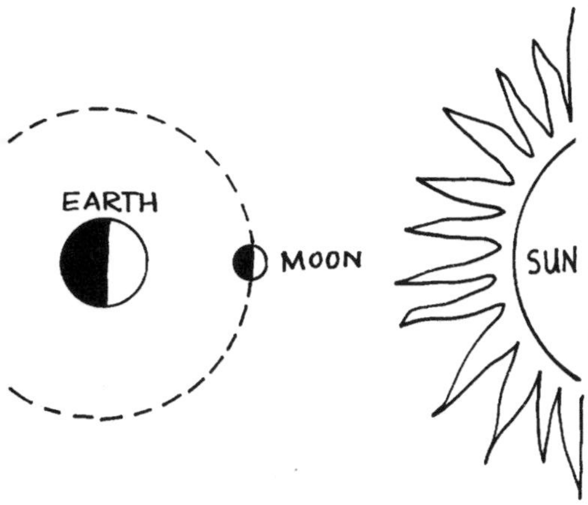

For 22–32, fill in the word that is being defined.

_____ 22. type of rock formed by volcanic activity

_____ 23. planet noted for thousands of rings

_____ 24. largest planet; has cloud bands and red spot

_____ 25. scale used to measure earthquakes

_____ 26. outermost layer of Earth

_____ 27. usually farthest known planet from sun

_____ 28. billions of stars held together by gravity

_____ 29. objects orbiting sun between Mars & Jupiter

_____ 30. agency that oversees U.S. space program

_____ 31. 3 agents of erosion

_____ 32. theory explaining moving of continents and internal Earth processes

Name _____

For 33-35, use the diagram below to answer the questions.

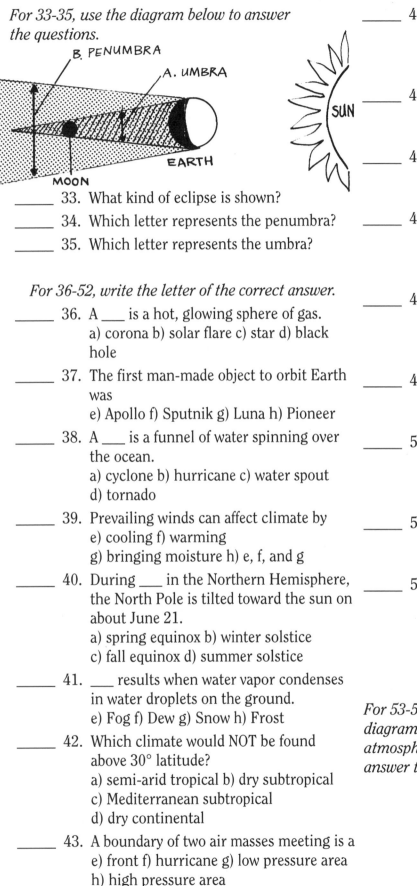

_____ 33. What kind of eclipse is shown?

_____ 34. Which letter represents the penumbra?

_____ 35. Which letter represents the umbra?

For 36-52, write the letter of the correct answer.

_____ 36. A ___ is a hot, glowing sphere of gas.
a) corona b) solar flare c) star d) black hole

_____ 37. The first man-made object to orbit Earth was
e) Apollo f) Sputnik g) Luna h) Pioneer

_____ 38. A ___ is a funnel of water spinning over the ocean.
a) cyclone b) hurricane c) water spout d) tornado

_____ 39. Prevailing winds can affect climate by
e) cooling f) warming
g) bringing moisture h) e, f, and g

_____ 40. During ___ in the Northern Hemisphere, the North Pole is tilted toward the sun on about June 21.
a) spring equinox b) winter solstice
c) fall equinox d) summer solstice

_____ 41. ___ results when water vapor condenses in water droplets on the ground.
e) Fog f) Dew g) Snow h) Frost

_____ 42. Which climate would NOT be found above 30° latitude?
a) semi-arid tropical b) dry subtropical
c) Mediterranean subtropical
d) dry continental

_____ 43. A boundary of two air masses meeting is a
e) front f) hurricane g) low pressure area
h) high pressure area

_____ 44. A ___ is a reusable craft for transporting people & equipment into space.
a) space probe b) rocket c) space shuttle
d) space station

_____ 45. Which does NOT make water more dense?
e) higher salt content f) colder temperatures g) melting ice h) great evaporation

_____ 46. Which is NOT a feature of the sun?
a) chromosphere b) corona c) photosphere d) quasar e) solar flares

_____ 47. The moon is ___ when it is less than ¼ visible and getting smaller
f) waxing crescent g) waning gibbous
h) waning crescent i) waxing gibbous

_____ 48. A wave in water less deep than ½ its wavelength is a ___ .
a) tidal wave b) shallow-water wave
c) upwelling d) deep-water wave

_____ 49. A ___ is a briefly visible meteor.
e) meteorite f) shooting star g) asteroid
h) comet

_____ 50. ___ are the prevailing winds in 30°–60° latitude in the Northern Hemisphere.
a) Trade winds b) Doldrums c) Easterlies
d) Westerlies

_____ 51. Which of these do NOT influence climate?
e) latitude f) longitude g) altitude
h) topography

_____ 52. The motion of an object relative to the position of its observer is ___ .
a) apparent motion b) real motion
c) rotation d) retrograde motion

For 53-56, use the diagram of Earth's atmosphere to answer these.

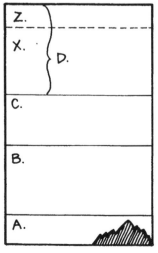

Name _____

_____ 53. Which letter represents the stratosphere?

_____ 54. Which layer is labeled D?

_____ 55. Which layer is the mesosphere?

_____ 56. In which layer does weather take place?

For 57-62, write the answer.

_____ 57. What wind blows from land to sea at night?

_____ 58. What do comets orbit?

_____ 59. What part of Earth's atmosphere absorbs harmful ultraviolet rays?

_____ 60. What causes surface currents on the ocean?

_____ 61. Which is more dense: cold or warm ocean water?

_____ 62. What kind of a front is pictured below?

For 63–67, write the word that is being defined.

_____ 63. fog mixed with pollution

_____ 64. the outer, incomplete shadow formed during an eclipse

_____ 65. magma that is released at Earth's surface during volcanic eruptions

_____ 66. thick mass of ice in motion

_____ 67. water that falls to Earth's surface from the atmosphere as rain, snow, hail, or sleet

For 68–72, use the diagram below.

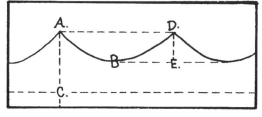

_____ 68. What part of the wave is A?

_____ 69. Which letter is at the wave base?

_____ 70. What does the distance A-D represent?

_____ 71. Which letter is in the trough?

_____ 72. What does the distance D-E represent?

For 73-74, use the diagram below.

_____ 73. Which diagram below pictures a spring tide?

_____ 74. Which diagram below pictures a neap tide?

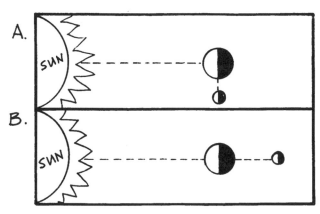

For 75–95, fill in the letter of the correct answer.

_____ 75. The ___ is the distance between the crests of two successive waves.
a) wave height b) wave period c) wavelength d) wave base

_____ 76. The area between two tidal bulges is ___ .
e) low tide f) spring tide g) high tide h) trough

_____ 77. A ___ occurs when the moon, sun, and Earth are aligned, with the moon on the opposite side of Earth from the sun.
a) new moon b) full moon c) first quarter d) third quarter moon

_____ 78. In a(n) ___ , water is under pressure from the weight of water in an aquifer in the layers above.
e) geyser f) sinkhole g) permeable rock h) artesian well

Name _____

Basic Skills/Earth & Space Science 6-8+

_____ 79. The difference between the highest and lowest tide is the ___ .
a) tidal range b) spring tide c) neap tide d) bulge

_____ 80. Precipitation that returns to the ocean is ___ .
e) a flood f) rain g) runoff h) water vapor

_____ 81. When Earth, moon, and sun are aligned, which is NOT happening?
a) neap tide b) spring tide c) high tides are highest d) low tides are lowest

_____ 82. The distance between the crest of a wave and the wave base is equal to ½ of ___ .
e) the wavelength f) the wave period g) the wave base h) the wave width

_____ 83. Which is NOT associated with wind erosion?
a) loess b) dune c) talus d) deflation

_____ 84. Which is a cause of tides?
e) winds f) gravitational force g) temperature changes h) ocean storms

_____ 85. The ___ is the steeply sloping edge of the continental shelf.
a) abyssal plain b) seamount c) continental slope d) ocean basin

_____ 86. ___ is the slow, downslope movement of earth material.
e) rockfalls f) mudflows g) deflation h) creep

_____ 87. A ___ is a funnel-shaped depression in the ground caused when limestone dissolves along cracks
a) stalactite b) sinkhole c) cave d) fumarole

_____ 88. The original hollow in which snow accumulates to form a valley glacier is a ___ .
e) cirque f) moraine g) oxbow lake h) striation

_____ 89. Which term(s) are associated with glaciers?
a) flow b) piedmont c) outflow d) crevasse e) cirque f) all of these

_____ 90. Which feature is not ordinarily used to identify a mineral?
g) hardness h) shape of crystals i) luster j) melting point k) streak l) mass m) smell

_____ 91. The ___ is the point on Earth's surface where the seismic activity is strongest in an earthquake.
a) focus b) fracture c) epicenter d) fold

_____ 92. Which group of rocks are rocks changed by high temperature and pressure?
e) metamorphic f) sedimentary g) igneous h) f and g

_____ 93. A geographic feature formed when a volcano erupts and the peak collapses into the hole created is a ___ .
a) dome b) cinder cone c) magma flow d) caldera

_____ 94. Which is (are) NOT igneous rock(s)?
e) limestone f) basalt g) pumice h) marble i) e and h j) f and h

_____ 95. Sediment carried along by river or stream (not dragged) is ___ .
a) runoff b) channel c) suspended load d) bedload

For 96-100, write the number of the feature from the diagram below.

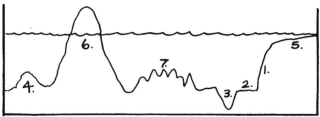

_____ 96. seamount

_____ 97. continental shelf

_____ 98. ocean trench

_____ 99. abyssal plain

_____ 100. continental slope

SCORE: Total Points _____ out of a possible 100 points

Name _____

EARTH & SPACE SCIENCE
SKILLS TEST ANSWER KEY

1. m
2. f
3. g
4. j
5. s
6. a
7. r
8. t
9. b
10. k
11. n
12. q
13. i
14. p
15. h
16. l
17. o
18. c
19. d
20. e
21. new
22. igneous
23. Saturn
24. Jupiter
25. Richter
26. crust

27. Pluto
28. galaxy
29. asteroids
30. NASA
31. any 3 of these: water, wind, gravity, ice
32. plate tectonics
33. lunar
34. B
35. A
36. c
37. f
38. c
39. h
40. d
41. f
42. a
43. e
44. c
45. g
46. d
47. g
48. b
49. f
50. d

51. f
52. a
53. B
54. thermosphere
55. C
56. A
57. land breeze
58. sun
59. ozone layer
60. wind
61. cold
62. warm
63. smog
64. penumbra
65. lava
66. glacier
67. precipitation
68. crest
69. C
70. wavelength
71. B
72. wave height
73. B
74. A
75. c

76. e
77. b
78. h
79. a
80. g
81. a
82. e
83. c
84. f
85. c
86. h
87. b
88. e
89. f
90. j
91. c
92. e
93. d
94. i
95. c
96. 4
97. 5
98. 3
99. 2
100. 1

Basic Skills/Earth & Space Science 6-8+

ANSWERS

Page 10

Features given may vary.
Order of planets:
1. Mercury / 0 moons / 2nd smallest, heavily cratered, dark color
2. Venus / 0 moons / cloud cover, yellow color
3. Earth / 1 moon / water vapor atmosphere, sustains life
4. Mars / 2 moons / polar caps, craters, clouds & fog, red color
5. Jupiter / 20 known moons / largest planet, gaseous, reddish-brown & white cloud bands, large red spot
6. Saturn / 17 moons / gaseous, many rings
7. Uranus / 15 moons / gaseous, dark rings
8. Neptune / 2 moons / gaseous, rings
9. Pluto / 1 moon / made of frozen water and gases

Bottom:
1. elliptical
2. aphelion
3. perihelion
4. Mars & Jupiter
5. Mercury, Venus, Earth, Mars
6. Jupiter, Saturn, Uranus, Neptune, Pluto

Page 11

Student-drawn solar systems may vary some. Check to see that planets are in the right order, have accurate coloring, and are drawn with accurate proportions.

Page 12

1. MY
2. P
3. MY
4. P
5. J
6. E
7. V
8. U
9. J
10. V
11. V
12. J
13. S
14. E
15. P
16. M
17. E
18. M
19. E
20. N
21. J
22. U
23. M
24. S
25. P
26. N
27. V
28. U
29. S
30. M
31. V
32. S
33. J

Page 13

1. quasar
2. red supergiant
3. sunspots
4. nebulae
5. star
6. pulsar
7. neutron star
8. galaxy
9. constellation
10. nova
11. photosphere
12. binary stars
13. black dwarf
14. Sirius A
15. supernova
16. white dwarf
17. variable star
18. Andromeda
19. Milky Way
20. corona
21. solar flares
22. black hole
23. chromosphere

Page 14

1. nucleus
2. shooting star
3. meteorite
4. Ceres
5. fireball
6. coma
7. asteroid belt
8. comets
9. comet's tail
10. meteor
11. asteroids
12. meteoroids
13. Halley's comet
14. the sun
15. away from the sun
16. elliptical

Page 15

Retrograde: apparent westward movement of a planet as seen from Earth
Real motion: actual movement of an object
Apparent motion: motion of an object relative to the position of its observer
Rotation: turning motion of an object on its axis
Revolution: circling of one object around another
Earth's gravity: attraction of object to Earth
Sun's gravity: attraction of object to the sun

1. day and night
2. about 24 hrs
3. Copernicus
4. rotation and revolution
5. seasons
6. 1 year/365 days

Page 16

1. seasons
2. summer
3. fall equinox; spring equinox
4. summer solstice
5. winter solstice
6. summer
7. winter solstice
8. spring equinox; fall equinox
9. summer solstice
10. 24 hours of
  1. spring equinox
  2. summer solstice
  3. fall equinox
  4. winter solstice

Page 17

1. C
2. F
3. A
4. E
5. D
6. H
7. B
8. G
9. D
10. G
11. A
12. E
13. C
14. H
15. F
16. B

Page 18

1. F
2. F
3. F
4. T
5. T
6. T
7. T
8. T
9. T
10. T
11. F
12. T
13. F
14. F
15. F
16. F
17. F
18. T
19. T
20. T

See that students have accurately labeled the diagrams of the eclipses.

Page 19

1. spectroscope
2. space shuttle
3. refracting
4. telescope
5. space lab
6. space station
7. reflecting
8. Apollo program
9. Gemini
10. space probe
11. moon walk
12. NASA
13. graph
14. thrust
15. radio telescope
16. rocket
17. satellite
18. Mercury
Mystery: Challenger Space Shuttle

Pages 20-21

1. 1971
2. 1958
3. 1964
4. 1990
5. 1973
6. 1984
7. 1965
8. 1903
9. 1986
10. 1959
11. 1959
12. 1976
13. 1986
14. 1974
15. 1988
16. 1960
17. 1926
18. 1962
19. 1966
20. 1961
21. 1968
22. 1968
23. 1973
24. 1965
25. 1977
26. 1983
27. 1996
28. 1957
29. 1961
30. 1969
31. 1981
32. 1957
33. 1962
34. 1963
35. 1965
36. 1966
37. 1970
38. 1966

Page 22

1-2. See that students have accurately labeled diagram as shown.

3. a. TR
   b. S
   c. M
   d. TH
   e. TR
   f. S

g. EX
h. TR
i. TPP
j. S
k. TH
l. I
m. TPP
n. TH
o. S
p. TPP
q. M
r. I
4. nitrogen, oxygen, argon, carbon dioxide, water vapor, traces of other gases
5. Ozone absorbs harmful ultraviolet radiation.
6. The force of air pressing down on Earth's surface
7. because of differences in air's density
8. no

Page 23

1. trade winds
2. doldrums
3. prevailing westerlies
4. cyclone
5. sea breeze
6. polar easterlies
7. hurricane
8. gale
9. the jet stream
10. front
11. land breeze
12. tornado
13. water spout
14. blizzard

Page 24-25

1. lows
2. dew
3. fog
4. tornado
5. rain
6. snow
7. lightning
8. fronts
9. cold air
10. highs
11. clouds
12. hail
13. frost
14. hurricane
15. thunder
16. wind
17. rainbows
18. precipitation
19. warm air
20. relative humidity

21. dew point
22. stationary front
23. anticyclone
24. tornado warning
25. temperature inversion
26. cyclones
27. tornado watch
28. sleet
29. blizzard
30. drought
31. cold front
32. warm front

Page 26

A. stationary
B. occluded
C. cold
D. warm
1. warm
2. cold
3. warm
4. dense
5. cold
6. cirrus
7. stratus
8. nimbostratus
9. rain
10. snow
11. cold
12. warm
13. cold
14. warm
15. cumulonimbus
16. cumulus
17. rain storms
18. cooler
19. clear
20. stops moving
21. several days
22. precipitation
23. cool
24. warm
25. wind
26. precipitation

Page 27

Answers will vary somewhat.
latitude—climates are cooler farther away from the equator
revolution—seasons change with Earth's closeness to sun
tilt of Earth—climate warmer when Earth tilts toward sun
water—milder, sometimes wetter effects
ocean currents—can warm or cool land, depending on the current temperatures

altitude—colder temperatures, affects precipitation
topography—causes variations in temperatures, winds, & moisture
land masses—tends toward colder, drier, hotter, or more extreme climates
prevailing winds—can cool or warm, depending on the wind
ice surfaces—cool temperatures
cultural factors—cities can increase pollution or humidity

pages 28-29

1. highland or polar
2. dry tropical
3. humid continental
4. dry tropical or subtropical
5. temperate marine
6. dry continental
7. no
8. dry continental
9. wet tropical
10. yes
11. wet-dry tropical
12. subarctic
13. humid continental
14. no

Page 30

A. surface current—movement of water caused by wind
B. density current—movement of water from areas of more to less density
C. waves—movement in which water rises and falls regularly
D. tides—shallow water waves caused by gravitational forces of the sun, moon, and Earth
E. upwellings—rising of cold, deep water toward the surface
F. tsunami—sea waves caused by earthquake activity
G. surf—result of the forming and breaking of many waves
1. nutrients
2. winds
3. tides

4. clockwise
5. counterclockwise
6. cooler temperatures
7. warmer temperatures
8. density currents
9. temperature; salinity
10. increase
11. density current
12. more
13. more
14. less
15. less
16. tsunamis
17. surf

Page 31

1. A, D
2. A, B, C, D, E, G
3. H, F
4. trough
5. wavelength
6. C, E
7. H, F
8. D, G
9. wave period
10. wavelength
11. rise and fall of water
12. in a circular motion
13. waves are slowed, get higher, curve over their tops, and break
14. tsunami
15. deep-water wave

Page 32

1. full moon spring tide: The moon, Earth, and sun are lined up with Earth between the sun and moon. The lined-up gravitational force pulls on bulge on the side of Earth towards the moon and the side opposite the moon causing spring tides. The high tides are highest during spring tide, and the low tides are lowest, giving the greatest tidal range.
2. new moon spring tide: The moon, Earth, and sun are lined up with moon between Earth and the sun. The lined-up gravitational force pulls on bulge on the side of Earth towards the moon and the side opposite the moon causing spring tides. The high tides

are highest during spring tide, and the low tides are lowest, giving the greatest tidal range.
3. third quarter neap tide: The moon is in the third quarter position, forming a right angle with Earth and the sun. The gravitational forces are not all pulling together, so the tides are minimal.
4. first quarter neap tide: The moon is in the first quarter position, forming a right angle with Earth and the sun. The gravitational forces are not all pulling together, so the tides are minimal.

Page 33

1. low tide
2. angle
3. bulge
4. first
5. tidal range
6. align
7. spring tides
8. high tides
9. third
10. lowest
11. semidiurnal
12. neap tides
13. full
14. diurnal
15. twice
16. new
Vertical: moon's gravitational force

Page 34

1. D....S, Z
2. A....T
3. F....U
4. G....V
5. E....W
6. B....X
7. C....Y

Page 35

1-4. wind, water, ice, gravity
Bottom:
1. disintegration
2. gravity
3. erosion
4. oasis
5. talus
6. dune

Answers

7. loess
8. mudflows
9. slump
10. abrasion
11. landslides
12. rockfalls
13. deflation
14. decomposition
15. weathering
16. creep

Page 36
1. velocity
2. drainage basin
3. bed load
4. suspended load
5. meandering
6. channel
7. flood plain
8. runoff
9. impermeable
10. permeable
11. sediment
12. alluvial fans
13. drainage system
14. delta

Page 37
1. NO...Caspian Sea
2. NO...mouth
3. NO...drainage system
4. NO...floodplain
5. NO...delta
6. YES
7. YES
8. YES
9. YES
10. NO...waterfall
11. NO...tributaries flow into rivers
12. YES
13. YES
14. NO...mouth
15. YES

Page 38
Jocelyn has these wrong: 2, 5, 6, 13
Her final score is 80%.

Page 39
1-6
2-14
3-25
4-18
5-39
6-1
7-38
8-20
9-46
10-27
11-37
12-44
13-34
14-2
15-30
16-42
17-33
18-4
19-40
20-8
21-43
22-41
23-36
24-29
25-3
26-45
27-10
28-31
29-24
30-15
31-28
32-35
33-17
34-13
35-32
36-23
37-11
38-7
39-5
40-19
41-22
42-16
43-21
44-12
45-26
46-9

Page 40
1. crust
2. MOHO (Mohorovicic Discontinuity)
3. mantle
4. yes
5. upper mantle
6. line between mantle and core
7. inner core
8. outer core
9. an ocean
10. mantle

Page 41
1. Sahara Desert...1410 ft
2. Asia...174,00,000 square miles
3. Indonesia...685 square miles
4. Mt. Everest...29,022 ft
5. Mt. Guallatiri (in Chile)...19,882 ft
6. Lambert Glacier...Antarctic
7. South Africa...12,467 ft
8. Greenland...840,000 square miles
9. 3800 million years
10. Great Barrier Reef...1200 miles
11. Caspian Sea...146,100 square miles
12. Angel Falls...3212 ft
13. 112 ft
14. Mammoth Caves...350 miles
15. Dead Sea...1286 ft
16. Marianas...35,837 ft
17. Pacific...64,000,000 square ft
18. 278 ft

pages 42-43
1. igneous, metamorphic, sedimentary
2. igneous
3. pumice
4. geodes
5. nonfoliated
6. harden
7. igneous
8. fossils
9. ripple marks
10. metamorphic
11. sandstone, limestone, shale, siltstone
12. foliated
13. sedimentary
14. dark
15. metamorphic, sedimentary
16. clastic
17. intrusive
18. slate, marble, quartzite, anthracite
19. sedimentary
20. granite, pumice, feldspar, basalt, felsite
21. nonclastic
22. anthracite
23. extrusive
24. compaction
25. cementation
26. conglomerate
27. breccia
28. shale
29. caves
30. corals

pages 44-45
Answers may vary somewhat.
1. no
2. no
3. feldspar
4. bauxite
5. graphite
6. no
7. gypsum
8. sulfur
9. yes
10. talc
11. halite (salt)
12. calcite
13. quartz
14. yes
15. chromite
16. fluorite
17. corundum (sapphire)
18. yes
19. no
20. yes
21. no
22. yes

Page 46
1. cinder cone
   Example B
2. stratovolcano
   Example C
3. shield
   Example D
4. dome Example A

Page 47
Clues may vary somewhat; should generally follow definitions below.

DOWN
1. troughs (downward folds) between folds in Earth's crust
2. scientists who study earthquakes and seismic activity
4. vibrations caused by sudden movement of surface rocks
5. strength of an earthquake
6. point on surface where seismic activity is strongest
7. ridges; upward fold in Earth's crust
10. breaks in rocks

ACROSS
3. vibrations resulting when a rock suddenly breaks and moves
8. seismic sea wave
9. bends in rock layers
10. point on fault deep below surface where movement occurs
11. measure of how much damage an earthquake causes
12. fractures along which movement takes place
13. instrument that records earthquakes
14. scale that measures earthquake magnitude
15. significant fault which runs most the length of California

Page 48
1-15
2-16
3-18
4-20
5-22
6-12
7-19
8-14
9-13
10-17
11-21
12-6
13-9
14-8
15-1
16-2
17-10
18-3
19-7
20-4
21-11
22-5

Page 49
Information students gather will vary according to reference materials used.

Page 50
1. G caldera
2. C geyser
3. A hot springs
4. H mudspots
5. B fumorale
6. I solfataras
7. J batholith
8. F sinkhole
9. D laccolith
10. K dike
11. E volcanic neck